THE BEGINNERS GUIDE TO
SHOTOKAN KARATE

GICHIN FUNAKOSHI
The father of modern day karate, who was a scholar of the Chinese classics as well as a karate master, was born in Shuri, Okinawa Prefecture, in 1868 and died in Tokyo in 1957.

The Beginners Guide to
SHOTOKAN
KARATE

by
John van Weenen
6th Dan

Chief Instructor:
Traditional Association of Shotokan Karate

First published November 1983
First Reprint April 1984
Second Reprint October 1985
Third Reprint August 1986
Fourth Reprint May 1987
Fifth Reprint January 1988
Sixth Reprint April 1989
Seventh Reprint December 1990
Eighth Reprint July 1991
Ninth Reprint July 1992
Tenth Reprint July 1993

The author would like to thank the following
instructors for their assistance:
Gursharan Sahota 4th Dan.
Bernard Coppen 3rd Dan.
John Caves 3rd Dan.
Andy Kidby 3rd Dan.
Roy Hazelwood 3rd Dan.
Christopher Burton 3rd Dan.
Jane van Weenen 3rd Dan.
Also Eddie McClagish, T.A.S.K. General Secretary
for his help with the revised edition.

ISBN NO 0 9517660 0 7
© Copyright 1983 John van Weenen

Published by John van Weenen, Fineshade Abbey, Fineshade, Northants NN17 3BB, UK.
Distributed by Biblios Publishers' Distribution Services Ltd, Star Road, Partridge Green,
West Sussex RH13 8LD. Telephone 0403 710971, Facsimile 0403 711143
Printed by White Crescent Press Ltd, Crescent Road, Luton LU2 0AG

I dedicate this book to my wife Jane

CONTENTS

PREFACE

The reasons that led me to write this book are many. However, the overriding and deciding factor was the beginner's need for an elementary instruction manual that covered the three basic aspects of karate training, written by a westerner for westerners.

The majority of books on the market today have been written by Japanese, and quite rightly so, for in my opinion they are better qualified to write and teach Karate-Do than any other people. Having said that, in my experience over the last 20 years, many books have tended to be a little overpowering for the average beginner. Consequently, he learns very little from them.

I hope "The Beginner's Guide to Shotokan Karate" will rectify this. It is intended as a manual to assist club training and to enable the beginner to follow the basic fundamentals that he has been taught by his own teacher. Of course technique will differ from instructor to instructor, each having his own "Body System", but by and large Shotokan is universal in its basic concepts, and the reader should bear this in mind when comparing techniques.

As a traditionalist, I feel some measure of responsibility in the continuance of Karate-Do as a way of life, not merely as a sport, for I feel if the art has survived since the sixth century, it *must* be good and have a great deal to offer, otherwise it would have disappeared a long time ago.

May I take this opportunity of thanking Mr Alan Cooke who so painstakingly took the many photographs and without whose help this book would not have been possible.

John van Weenen
November 1983

1

A BEGINNERS VIEW

I came to Karate by chance. Oh I had from time to time observed groups of exponents in various positions of self-defence, and my son was a keen participant, but it never occurred to me that here was an activity with which I would become involved, let alone enthralled by. As a lapsed sportsman of approaching middle years, it was the organised keep fit that first attracted me — the twenty-minute warm-up period that, under the guidance of trained experts, systematically and scientifically stretched and toned up all the muscles and sinews of the body.

I soon discovered, almost without realising the fact, that I had entered into the spirit of Karate, and having come to terms with the early movements, I became aware of a re-awakening of a forgotten boyhood emotion — anticipation. As I looked forward to each new lesson, I would practise at home in front of the bathroom mirror.

It was at this stage, however, that I became a little frustrated. My problems, in common with others no doubt, were two-fold. Firstly in remembering the sequence of previously taught movements, and secondly, being a less than gifted linguist, in grasping the Japanese commands and terminology. As a consequence I was forever Gyaku-tzuki-ing when I should have been Mae-geri-ing.

My disappointment was in being unable to find any suitable publication, aimed at the beginner, that supplemented the lessons of the Dojo, was written in basic Western terms, explained simply and pictorially the movements, and served as a quick yet comprehensive guide. Life, however, is very much about being in the right place at the right time. For me to have come to the sport under the guidance of Sensei van Weenen was indeed a stroke of good fortune, and when he asked me to assist him in producing such a book, aimed primarily for the benefit of the beginner, I was naturally delighted.

My observation is that Karate brings untold benefits to its fortunate exponents — confidence, physical fitness, self-defence, and so much more. By its very teachings it instils the virtues of honour and consideration, encouraging always a greater awareness of one's fellow creatures, and a genuine desire to leave only pleasant and fond memories as one journeys along "The Way".

If this book assists in achieving any of these objectives it will have provided a worthwhile service to the individual, and have been of benefit to Karate Do.

Left: In the Dojo — Sensei and student.   Paul Hooley, 1983.

FOREWORD

John van Weenen is well suited to author this book on Shotokan Karate, having trained for twenty years with the great names of the style. John is one of the few Westerners who can appreciate that there is more to Karate than the purely physical. The very use he makes of the word "Traditional" in the title of his own association confirms that he is devoted to the deeper aspects of this fascinating art. It is so very important, when learning Karate, to understand that it is more than just an impressive physical system; it is a deep philosophy and a unique expression of the Japanese warrior spirit. To teach the techniques without the underlying meaning and significance is only to graze the surface.

I well remember my teachers patiently explaining the importance of attitude to training; the need to train and constantly return to basics. It is only by constantly practising the basic techniques of Karate that the student can learn to react instinctively. The proper practice of Karate – as described in John's excellent book – leaves the mind calm and relaxed. It becomes cleared of the clutter of preconceptions and "when to do what". Having reached this stage, the person is truly competent.

I see so many Karate students today who believe that success in competition is the be all and end all of Karate. To be sure, the sporting aspect is healthy and enjoyable, but it is not the major part of Karate. The original idea behind Karate was not to win competitions; not even to be effective in self-defence (though Karate certainly produces this effectively), but to develop the character and mind of the student. The true Karateka is, unfortunately, a rare beast in this day and age. We have embraced the actions but not the philosophy. John van Weenen is a true Karateka and, consequently, his work is all the more important to those who are following the "Way". It is not just another manual; it is a well written, concise insight into Shotokan Karate – a major school of Japanese Karate.

David Mitchell

Secretary Martial Arts Commission.
Secretary British Karate Federation.
Secretary of English Karate Council.
Member of Directing Committee of European Karate Union.
Member of Directing Committee of World Union of Karate Organisations.

November 1983

KARATE
YESTERDAY AND TODAY

Present day Karate can be traced directly back to the time of Daruma, the Founder of Zen Buddhism. About 1400 years ago, he left Western India on foot for China to give lectures on Buddhism.

His journey of several thousand miles was perilous to say the least, for he had to cross the Himalayas, unbridged rivers, as well as vast stretches of wilderness. He made his journey alone, which gives us a clue to his spiritual as well as physical strength.

In later years, Daruma introduced to his many followers a system of physical movements to improve their strength, following a journey to the Shao-Lin Temple when most of them fell by the way-side from exhaustion.

With this system the Monks of the Shao-Lin Temple came to be known throughout China for their courage and fortitude.

In later times it came to be known as Shorin-Ji Kempo, and this method eventually reached the Ryukyu Islands and developed into Okinawa-Te, the forerunner of present day Karate.

The two Okinawan Masters, Azato and Itosu, were most responsible for teaching and influencing Funakoshi – the father of modern day Karate.

Karate was first introduced to the Japanese public in 1922, when Funakoshi, who was then Professor at the Okinawa Teacher's College, was invited to lecture and demonstrate at an exhibition of Traditional Martial Arts sponsored by the Ministry of Education. His demonstration so impressed the audience that he was flooded with requests to teach in Tokyo.

Instead of returning to Okinawa, Funakoshi taught Karate at various universities, and in 1936 established the Shotokan, a great landmark in the history of Karate in Japan.

In 1955 the Japan Karate Association came into being with Funakoshi as its chief instructor.

Over the years, many of Funakoshi's students have become teachers and masters in their own right, so we see the formation of various styles of Karate, each group basically following Funakoshi's teachings, with its leader developing his own style and technique in accordance with his own "Body System".

Karate has spread to almost every country in the civilised world. It is gaining in popularity everywhere, not only as a Martial Art and Self Defence, but also as a competitive sport.

The latter worries me, for I cannot help feeling that when the J.K.A. arranged and held the first All Japan Karate Championships in 1957, thus putting sport Karate on the map, they had unwittingly grasped the (Shotokan) Tiger by its tail!

INTRODUCTION
BASIC TECHNIQUES

The fundamental techniques of Karate are punching, striking, blocking and kicking, and certain considerations need to be observed before they can be performed effectively.

The following factors should be taken into account:

Form – Balance – Centre of Gravity.
Concentration of Power.
Rhythm.
Timing.
Hara – Hips.

Form: Correct form is very important in the execution of Karate techniques as the body must harmonize in order to acquire the stability necessary to sustain the shock of delivering a kick or punch.

Balance: Good balance is essential when performing any Karate technique, especially kicks. At times the body's whole weight must be supported on one leg or transferred quickly from one leg to the other.

Centre of Gravity: Involves Hara, the body's physical and spiritual centre of gravity. Any technique no matter what direction must keep the Hara at a constant level. For example whilst performing Oi Zuki, if at the halfway stage the legs are straightened causing the Hara to rise, and then lowered as the punch is completed, the full power of the technique will not be propelled in a forward direction (towards the opponent).

Concentration of Power: When performing basic techniques the body should remain relaxed and only tensed at the end of the movement when contact is made. This tension is known as "Kime" or focus. Physics dictate that a muscle that is contracted cannot move as quickly as one that is relaxed. Both muscles and tendons should be kept relaxed to allow instant response to changing circumstances. "Kime" is often misunderstood as being "Tensing". "Kime" is relaxing, tensing at the appropriate time and then relaxing.

Rhythm: Is essential in most sports. Think of the poetry of the hurdler or perhaps the butterfly swimmer for example.

In Karate, rhythm is more noticeable in "Kata" and some Karateka have better rhythm than others. Ultimately, a person's "Kinetic" sense is responsible for a Kata being good – or very good.

Rhythm keeps each technique in Kata separate, yet joins them harmoniously together as a whole.

Timing: Good timing is vital and if incorrect, will cause the technique to fail. A punch delivered too soon may be out of range and therefore rendered ineffective, whilst a punch delivered too late may result in no uncertain terms for the executor.

6

Hara: All body power should emanate from the Hara, the body's natural centre of gravity. If tension is only applied to the muscles of the forearm when punching, the punch will be weak, using only a fraction of the body's capability. Understanding the Hara is the single most important factor in the execution of Karate techniques, for without this knowledge the student will progress up to a point – and no further.

Hips: Coupled with Hara is the Hip movement or "Tanden". When performing basic techniques, the hips should rotate rather than undulate. Of course there are exceptions to this rule, as with some kicks, but by and large, the mechanics of the hip movement must be appreciated and the laws of action and reaction understood. The timing of the hips is crucial to the success of the technique.

PREVENTION OF LONG-TERM INJURY TO JOINTS

Prior to A.D. 1900, Karate development was a slow, gradual process which had spanned centuries. This all changed with the research and teachings of **Funakoshi Sensei** and the acceptance of Karate in Japan following his demonstration in Kyoto in 1915.

With the exception of several hundred American G.I.s after World War II had finished, virtually all the students of Karate between 1915 and 1960 were Oriental – more accurately, they were Japanese. The fact that they were shorter and more squat than their Western counterparts resulted in a difference in the mechanics of the techniques of punching, kicking, striking and blocking. This difference was not **understood immediately** by the Japanese instructors who brought Karate to the West.

Consequently, the long-limbed Westerners allowed their punches and kicks to terminate only when the arm or leg would not travel any further. Of course, we now know that "locking out" a punch or kick will aggravate the joint; so much so, that eventually it will become arthritic. The arm or leg must be stopped just short of its maximum travel by **utilising the appropriate muscles** to focus or "kime".

At present, there is no known cure for osteoarthritis, which affects the joints of many elderly people. Regular exercise through Karate training will help combat this affliction. Incorrect Karate training may hasten its approach. This point cannot be made too strongly.

KATA

Kata is the Japanese word meaning formal exercise and consists of a series of predetermined movements, offensive and defensive, performed consecutively in a set sequence.

The practitioner is fighting four or eight imaginary opponents and to the unenlightened observer, will sometimes resemble a form of shadow boxing.

Until thirty years ago, freestyle contests or engagement matches were unheard of and training consisted mainly of Kata practice. As a result of continually striving to perfect these techniques, Kata, being a contest with oneself, the spirit of Karate-Do prevailed, as it had done for centuries.

About 50 Kata's have come down to us to the present day, these were created by Masters of past generations. The "Type" of movements in the individual Kata gives us a clue to the physical makeup of the Master who created it.

It is probably true to say that Funakoshi did more to systemise the teaching of Kata than any other person.

Kata has many advantages, primarily enabling one to practice alone – anywhere, and without special equipment. As a method of all round exercise, it is almost unbeatable and provides a working knowledge of self defence techniques.

Truly the key to Karate-Do lies within the performance of Kata – and it's there for the taking.

KUMITE

Kumite is the training method where the techniques of defence and attack can be put to practical application. The advantage of training with a partner as opposed to oneself means that, given reasonable control, a student can develop his technique and "Kime" by physically blocking a strong attack.

Kumite training must follow a set pattern, proven over the years. As this book is intended for beginners to 4th Kyu Grade – the following types apply.

Go Hon Kumite – five attack sparring.

Sambon Kumite – three attack sparring.

Kihon Ippon Kumite – basic one attack sparring.

Kaeshi Ippon Kumite – basic one attack (Oi Zuki counter).

Jiyu Ippon Kumite – semi free one attack sparring.

Go Hon Kumite requires the proficiency of formal techniques.

Kihon Ippon Kumite teaches the ability to block and counter strongly – so developing Kime. It also teaches distancing (MAAI). Timing is improved by leaving the block and counter to the last minute.

Jiyu Ippon Kumite is the transitional stage between Kihon Ippon and Jiyu Kumite (free sparring), a complete subject on its own and not covered in this book.

PART 1 KIHON
BASIC TECHNIQUES

The following 84 pages deal exclusively with the more popular basic techniques of Punching, Striking, Blocking and Kicking. All of these techniques can be performed in one or other of the basic Shotokan stances.
As this book is intended for beginners up to 4th Kyu Grade, only the following stances need be mastered, but having said that, students should train hard and endeavour to develop strong stances, as they are mostly the basis for techniques to come.

Zenkutsu Dachi – Front stance.
A strong attacking stance with 70% of the body weight over the front leg.

Kōkutsu Dachi – Back stance.
Used mainly for blocking frontal attacks, having 70% of the body weight over the back leg.

Kiba Dachi – Straddle Leg stance.
Very effective when used in conjunction with side snap or thrust kicks, body weight is evenly spread between both legs.

Fudo Dachi – Rooted stance.
A very strong stance midway between Zenkutsu and Kiba Dachi. The body weight is slightly more forward then back.

Neko Ashi Dachi – Cat stance.
A beautiful stance mainly used in blocking. With 90% of the body weight over the back leg, this stance is ideal for kicking with the front leg.

Left: Shutō Uchi – the moment 10 concrete roof tiles shatter

PUNCHING

Theoretical Considerations for Punching

In basic training, most punches start from the hip but once they have been perfected it may be necessary to punch from any position. Karate punches, in the main, travel in a straight line – the shortest distance between two points – and in an ideal situation, the opposite arm should do the same, in a reverse direction of course. Twisting the wrist on contact aids focus and exhalation. The timing of the beginning of a punch is crucial. If the fist leaves the waist too soon, it will have a pushing effect into its target and be only as strong as the weight or momentum of the person punching allows. Correspondingly, should the punch leave the hip too late, it will never gather momentum in time for it to have any appreciable effect.

Class performing Lunge Punch – during outdoor training session

CHOKU ZUKI
STRAIGHT PUNCH

Choku Zuki is the most basic Karate punch and is learned in the Hachiji Dachi stance. The punching hand begins at the waist in the inverted position and travels in a straight line to the target. It stays relaxed, as does the rest of the body until just prior to the end of its travel, when it twists 180° and the whole body is tensed. The opposite arm moves in harmony with the punching arm but of course in the reverse direction. Contact is made with Seiken (Fore Fist).

Application

1

2

3

4

15

OI ZUKI
LUNGE PUNCH

Application

Oi Zuki is virtually the same as Choku Zuki but performed whilst stepping forward or back. Starting from the Gedan Barai position bring the rear leg up to the front leg, keeping them both bent at this point, and then carry on forward into the next Zenkutsu Dachi. The arms remain in almost the same position right until the end of the technique and then exchange places, thus utilising fully the snapping action of the arms. At this point, the hips should be square on, body tensed and breath exhaled.

1

2

3

4

GYAKU ZUKI
REVERSE PUNCH

Application

Gyaku Zuki is a technique, usually
performed on the spot, using the
reverse hand to deliver the punch. It is
possibly Karate's strongest punch,
relying very much on applying the
power generated by twisting the hips.
From the Yoi position in Zenkutsu
Dachi with the left hand open, commence
the punch and the withdrawal of the
left arm simultaneously. As in the
photographs opposite it is
important to keep the
hips still in the 45° position as well as
the body (Hanmi) until the second half
of the technique.
As the right hand turns over to punch so
the left inverts and at this point the right
hip is thrust forward to the maximum.
The breath is exhaled and the body
tensed.
The final action of the hands, arms, hips,
body, breathing and tension must
culminate simultaneously.

1

2

3

4

MOROTE ZUKI
DOUBLE PUNCH (AUGMENTED)

Application

Morote Zuki begins by having both hands inverted on their respective hips, and in this technique, both arms punch together. Either or both fists make contact – one punching, both punching, or one augmenting the other. During this technique both hips remain fully facing forward and again the body tensed, breath exhaled at the moment of contact.

1

2

3

4

AGE ZUKI
RISING PUNCH

Application

Age Zuki is a rising punch which makes use of the back of the fist and rises to contact the opponent UNDER the chin. It is performed in a similar way to the reverse punch, the main difference being, that the punching arm swings in a wide vertical arc.

As the technique nears its conclusion, the right (reverse) hip is thrust forward, the back leg is pushed back and the body tensed whilst exhaling via the mouth.

1

2

3

4

MAWASHI ZUKI
ROUNDHOUSE PUNCH

Mawashi Zuki may be performed as a stationary technique (Gyaku) or as a stepping punch depending on circumstances.
It follows an outward, circular rising path culminating in Seiken (Fore Fist) contacting the temple, at which time the hips should be rotated accordingly. The muscles should be tensed and exhalation takes place via the mouth.

Application

1

2

3

4

URA ZUKI
CLOSE PUNCH

Ura Zuki is a punch similar to Gyaku Zuki, except the punching arm remains bent on completion and the fist, inverted.

It travels in a straight line and the punch is complete when the punching arm elbow is about six inches from the hip.

Ura Zuki is a lovely "Close In" fighting technique when directed at the Solar Plexus.

Application

26

1

2

3

4

27

TATE ZUKI
VERTICAL PUNCH

Tate Zuki is usually performed as a reverse (Gyaku) technique similar again to Gyaku Zuki. The same straight line is followed but this time, the fist turns only 90° – a quarter turn – and on completion, the punching arm remains slightly bent at the elbow. Exhalation and Kime are the same as preceding techniques.

Application

1

2

3

4

YAMA ZUKI
U PUNCH

Yama Zuki is a simultaneous multi
level attack. From a left forward stance,
put the right inverted fist by the waist
and bring the left fist over the top of it,
keeping it vertical. From this beginning
position, direct the right fist upward
and forward in a semi-circular fashion
towards the opponent's face.
The right fist finishes with the back of
the fist up, having revolved 180°.
The left fist pushes forward and
inverted, attacks the solar plexus.
Both fists should reach the opponent
together, therefore they should remain
in a vertical line. A slight body
inclination is necessary.

Application

1

2

3

4

KAGE ZUKI
HOOK PUNCH

Kage Zuki is ideal as a close in fighting body punch but with the fist finishing up in line with your body, it is necessary to step into your opponent to ensure its effectiveness. Used a great deal in Tekki Kata's, this technique is usually performed in Kiba Dachi. Special attention should be given to Kime, especially to the Deltoids and Latissimus Dorsi.

Application

1

2

3

4

33

STRIKING

Theoretical Considerations for Striking

Striking techniques involve the snapping action of the elbow and rely a great deal on the laws of action and reaction for their power. The force exerted in a striking action is increased by the snapping back effect of the arm, allowing the power of the strike to continue unimpeded to, or through its target. The strike will only be effective if the striking action coincides with the correct application of hips, exhalation and focus. Most strikes serve admirably as blocks too.

Class performing Knife Hand Strike from Heian Yondan, during outdoor training session.

SHUTŌ UCHI
KNIFE HAND STRIKE
(OUTSIDE)

Shutō Uchi (outside) is a semi-circular
strike to the neck or temple using the
hand edge or "Knife Hand". As
illustrated above it can be performed as
a reverse technique or as a stepping
movement depending on Maai
(distancing). In both cases proper use
of the hips is essential.

Application

36

1

2

3

4

SHUTŌ UCHI
KNIFE HAND STRIKE (INSIDE)

Shutō Uchi (inside) uses the same part of the hand as the outside technique but commences its movement with the striking hand cupping the opposite ear and the body is practically sideways on at the conclusion of the technique. Contact areas are the neck or temple.

Application

38

1

2

3

4

TETTSUI UCHI
BOTTOM FIST STRIKE

Tettsui Uchi can be used to attack most parts of the body. In the case of being grabbed by the wrist, one can use the swinging action of the arm to break the grip and continue over the head, so attacking the opponents skull with Tettsui Uchi.

Application

1

2

3

4

URAKEN UCHI
BACK FIST STRIKE

Application

Uraken Uchi has basically two forms. The first employs a lateral, semi-circular snapping action focusing the back fist on the opponent's temple. The second involves a semi-circular, overhead strike concentrating the power of the back fist onto the opponent's nose.

The former is a favourite technique for the "Pogo People" for in tournaments, the speed at which it can score can be devastating. A good example of the second occurs in Heian San Dan – or Seienchin.

1

2

3

4

HAITO UCHI
RIDGE HAND STRIKE (OUTSIDE)

Haito Uchi or ridge hand strike makes use of the opposite side of the hand to Shutō Uchi. The target area is the temple but make sure the thumb is not protruding out too far otherwise it may get broken. The striking hand swings round the body in a circular motion from a palm up to a palm down position. The beginner should understand straight line techniques before he attempts Haito Uchi, if not, he allows his elbow to go outside the body line when performing basic punches.

Application

44

1

3

2

4

45

HAITO UCHI
RIDGE HAND STRIKE (INSIDE)

Haito Uchi (inside) is often performed from the straddle leg stance, the striking hand moves from palm down to the palm up position and the target area can be the face, temple or neck. On completion of this technique, the body is side on.

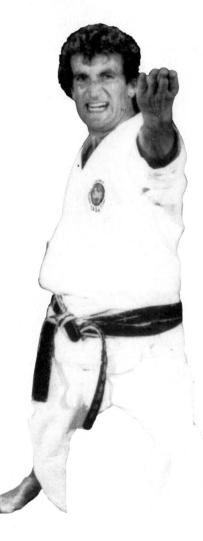

Application

1

2

3

4

JŌDAN EMPI UCHI
UPPER ELBOW STRIKE

Jōdan Empi Uchi. The effective attacking range is drastically reduced when using elbow attacks as opposed to punches or strikes. Therefore Empi techniques have to be for close encounters. Jōdan Empi Uchi is very similar to Age Uke in many ways – certainly the action and reaction principle is the same. On completion, the elbow should have contacted under the chin and have the back of the fist turned out. Good hip movement is important.

Application

1

2

3

4

49

CHŪDAN EMPI UCHI
MIDDLE ELBOW STRIKE

Chūdan Empi Uchi may be performed on the spot as a Gyaku technique or indeed practised as a stepping movement. Either way, the hip movement is of great importance and on completion the attackers index finger knuckle of his striking arm should fit into the small of his chest (touching sternum).

Application

1

2

3

4

51

USHIRO CHŪDAN EMPI UCHI
REVERSE MIDDLE ELBOW STRIKE

Application

Ushiro Chūdan Empi Uchi. When attacking in the Gyaku position as in the illustration, the left hip must be back as far as possible so aiding the attacking elbow. The right hand assists for augmenting purposes. It is important to have the left fist facing palm up and the right hip pushed as far forward as possible. The beginner, when practising his first punch, Choku Zuki, inadvertently performs a reverse elbow strike.

1

2

3

4

YOKO CHŪDAN EMPI UCHI
SIDE MIDDLE ELBOW STRIKE

Yoko Chūdan Empi Uchi is generally performed in the Kiba Dachi stance and the opponent's sternum makes a fine target for this penetrating technique. On completion, the back of the fist remains up and care should be taken to control very carefully when practising, as sternums have a nasty habit of breaking.

Application

1

2

3

4

BLOCKING

Theoretical Considerations for Blocking

Blocking consists of parrying or deflecting blows in such a way as to leave the defender unharmed, and in an advantageous position to counter attack successfully. The attacking limb will have its course altered by the influence of the blocking arm or leg moving in an upwards, downwards or sideways direction.

Advanced training class in progress (Chūdan Uchi Ude Uke)

AGE UKE
UPPER RISING BLOCK

Application

Age Uke is one of the most basic
Shotokan blocks. Points to
remember are these:
The blocking arm should rise
from the waist at an angle of 45°.
The arm and fist turn 180° at the
end of the technique as contact
is made. When pulling the
opposite arm down, make sure
the elbow pulls down in the
direction of the hip. On completion,
the hips and body must be 45° to the
front and the back leg must be
pushed straight on contact.

SOTO UDE UKE
OUTSIDE FOREARM BLOCK

Application

Soto Ude Uke is perhaps the strongest mid section block of all. On occasions it can be used to block kicks with surprising effectiveness.

The block starts its life at Jōdan level pulled well back past the head. It travels from that position, in a semi circle to a spot roughly in front of the chest and on completion, the wrist turns 180° just prior to Kime. Both body and hips turn 45° into Hanmi.

1

2

3

4

UCHI UDE UKE
INSIDE FOREARM BLOCK

Application

Uchi Ude Uke is a lot easier to perform than Soto Ude Uke as far as beginners are concerned. The blocking arm starts from above the opposite hip – back of the fist up – and swings in an arc across the body. It finishes its journey in line with the side of the body, the elbow being bent at a 90° angle and the top of the fist in line with the shoulder. The body and hips twist to the 45° position as the block is completed.

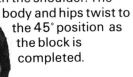

1

2

3

4

63

MOROTE UKE
AUGMENTED FOREARM BLOCK

Application

Morote Uke is an inside forward block augmented and strengthened by having the opposite arm to assist it. Indeed, the augmenting arm is quite interesting in so far as it hangs loosely by the side of the body, almost being left behind, then finally accelerates to catch the blocking arm up.

In touching the blocking arm just inside the elbow it strengthens the block quite considerably for it brings into play the muscles on that side of the body and promotes increased harmony.

1

2

3

4

SHUTO UKE
KNIFE HAND BLOCK

Application

Shutō Uke – This technique is more difficult than most, therefore it often gets neglected by beginner and high grade alike. Points to remember are: Keep the blocking arm at a 45° angle, otherwise, one may miss the punch completely. The opposite hand should strike the solar plexus as it pulls back. This will assist in Kime. Keep the body and hips at 45° and try not to let the back knee turn in.

1

2

3

4

TATE SHUTŌ
VERTICAL KNIFE HAND BLOCK

Application

Tate Shutō is a block utilising the knife hand edge. One needs to be a little more confident when using this technique as opposed to the more conventional blocks. However, once the student has become reasonably accurate, this block will begin to appeal more. It can be used to attack inside or outside an opponent's arm and prepares the way for a rapid counter punch.

1

2

3

4

JŪJI UKE
X BLOCK (JŌDAN)

Jūji Uke is a very strong double handed blocking technique that can be performed Jōdan or Gedan.
In this, the Jōdan version, the hands rise from the hips at 45° and lock together, crossed above the head. The technique, illustrated here, is called Haishu Jūji Uke, for the back of the hands make contact with the attacker's arm. If performed from a left forward stance, it is important to have the right hip forward as the block concludes.

Application

1

2

3

4

JŪJI UKE
X BLOCK (GEDAN)

Jūji Uke (Gedan) is a double block used in conjunction with the hips, to stop a front kick and simultaneously attack the shin bone. It really consists of two techniques – Gedan Barai and Tate Zuki. To ensure success, this block needs to be executed quickly, stopping the kicking leg in its tracks and preventing it from gaining speed and momentum.

Application

2

4

GEDAN BARAI
DOWNWARD BLOCK

Application

Gedan Barai – The most basic of blocks is probably used and practised more than any other technique. Usually performed in Zenkutsu Dachi, it makes maximum use of the arms, legs, body and hips. Most lessons involve many Gedan Barai's – it's the first technique from the very first Kata and it's still there in the most advanced one. Yes – the left Gedan Barai is most people's strongest block – what about the right one?

2

4

KAKIWAKE UKE
WEDGE BLOCK

Application

Kakiwake Uke, the last of our basic blocks is a wedge block, which, after training, is a very effective defence against being grabbed by the coat lapels. Its effective execution depends mainly on being able to contract the Hara and the muscles at the side of the body.

On completion, it leaves the attacker's body wide open and his position is extremely vulnerable, having both hands and arms outside yours.

1

2

3

4

KICKING

Theoretical Considerations for Kicking

Kicking uses the whole of one's body to the maximum and the hips especially play a major role in executing the various techniques. Basically, there are three types of kicks: Snap kicks, thrust kicks and striking kicks. In this book, we have tried to show a representative example from each group but have covered only the basic kicks needed by the beginner.

Snap kicks depend for their success on snapping the leg straight from the knee and then back again as quickly as possible. Once raised, the knee is used as a fulcrum for a semi-circular movement. Thrust kicks rely on raising the knee first and then thrusting the leg straight using the force of the hip for additional power.

Striking kicks may be used for blocking or attacking and their main virtue is flexibility. Balance is a key factor in kicking and keeping the sole of the supporting foot firmly on the floor ensures maximum stability.

A good tip is to aim the knee at the target – the foot should automatically follow.

Class performing Mawashi Geri during outdoor training session

MAE GERI
FRONT KICK

Mae Geri, a front kick performed from Zenkutsu Dachi is a snapkick acquiring its power from the snapping action of the lower leg aided by the application of the hips. Basically there are three positions that constitute this kick. Firstly, the kicking leg knee is raised in front and to the centre of the body. Secondly, the leg is straightened, hips applied, instep straightened and toes curled back.

Thirdly, the leg is snapped back assuming the first position and with the hips returned to *their* original position, the back should be straight and balance maintained.

Application

1

2

3

4

YOKO GERI KEAGE
SIDE SNAP KICK

Yoko Geri Keage is another snap kick but this time the kicking leg travels to the side of the body. Usually performed from a Kiba Dachi, the kicking leg knee is first raised to the side, then the leg is straightened and at this point, the hip rises up to augment the snapping action. Finally, the leg is snapped back – hip lowered and the stance resumed. The striking point is the foot edge (Sokuto).

Application

1

2

3

4

YOKO GERI KEKOMI
SIDE THRUST KICK

Yoko Geri Kekomi utilises the thrusting action of the leg augmented by the hip. It is more of a "Total Commitment" technique and requires good control and balance keeping the recovery factor in mind. As with Keage, the striking point is Sokuto. An important point to bear in mind is the pivoting action on the ball of the supporting foot as the thrusting takes place. Failure to do this could result in a damaged cartilage in the knee of that supporting leg.

Application

1

2

3

4

MAWASHI GERI
ROUNDHOUSE KICK

Mawashi Geri is a semi circular snap kick using the ball of the foot (Koshi) as the striking point. From a Zenkutsu Dachi, raise the knee sideways keeping the leg bent and the toes curled up. Then snap the leg forward aiming the foot at the target, at the same time allowing the hips to rotate. Immediately the leg has straightened, snap it back together

with the hips to their original position. At all times endeavour to keep the knee higher than the foot.

Application

1

2

3

4

USHIRO GERI
REVERSE KICK

Ushiro Geri makes use of the thrusting action of the leg, aided by the hips in a rearward direction. Usually performed as a spinning technique using the heel as a striking point, Ushiro Geri takes the face of the person kicking furthest away from the attacker and encourages him to commit himself to the technique much more. However, this commitment in competitions may result in disqualification through excessive contact. Both hips should be thrust back simultaneously, as in Oi Zuki or Mae Geri.

Application

1

2

3

4

URA MIKAZUKI GERI
CRESCENT KICK BLOCK

Ura-Mikazuki-Geri may be used as a block or an attack using the sole of the foot as a striking point. Endeavour to keep the knee parallel to the floor when performing this circular movement.

Application

1

2

4

MIKAZUKI GERI
CRESCENT KICK

Mikazuki Geri performed as a block or an attack utilises the ball of the foot (Koshi) and the kick takes its name from the crescent like action of the leg whether moving in an inward or outward direction. The thigh of the kicking leg should remain parallel to the floor if possible.

Application

1

2

3

4

USHIRO MAWASHI GERI
REVERSE ROUNDHOUSE KICK

Ushiro-Mawashi-Geri. This is a reverse roundhouse kick using the heel as the striking point. Some styles prefer to contact with the sole of the foot. This certainly is the case in tournaments for obvious reasons. Bring the kicking leg up and round, rotating the hips and body to enable the heel to make contact with the back of the neck or back area in the case of Chūdan.

Application

1

2

3

4

KARATE IS FOR EVERYONE FOR LIFE!

Young children training in Karate

ENJOYED BY YOUNG AND OLD ALIKE

Older children training in Karate

PART 2 KATA
FORMAL EXERCISE

Kata have been with us for a long time, probably since the Sixth Century. What is remarkable, is that they have endured to this day. True – the techniques may have changed somewhat over the years due to external pressures and influences from the great masters of the past, but the fact remains, they are practised for the same reasons today as they were them. In a nutshell – "The Perfection of Character".
Kata offers so much – to so many by way of physical and mental training.
All the Katas in this book have at least one thing in common – they all begin with defensive movements – to show humility, on the practitioner's part. Their influence overall through physical exercise and breath control directly affect longevity of life. This is borne out by the advanced age to which many masters live.
By continually striving to improve and perfect the techniques in Kata, a person's attitude, mind and character are indirectly improved. Another point often overlooked by many Karateka and one, more profound by far than any other, is this – "a student training in a Dojo, no matter what country, in 1983 could be training in the same techniques as his predecessor was 1,000 years before him. In these days of change and modernisation, how nice it is to be involved in an art *that has truly stood "The Test of Time"*.

The following ten elements of Kata as taught by Kanazawa Sensei, must be well practised and understood in order to obtain maximum benefit:

- **Yoi No Kisin** – the spirit of getting ready. The concentration of will and mind against the opponent as a preliminary to the movements of the Kata.
- **Inyo** – the active and passive. Always keeping in mind both attack and defence.
- **Chikara No Kyojaku** – the manner of using strength. The degree of power used for each movement and position in Kata.
- **Waza No Kankyu** – the speed of movement. The speed used for each movement and position in Kata.
- **Tai No Shinshuku** – the degree of expansion or contraction. The degree of expansion or contraction of the body in each movement and position in Kata.
- **Kokyu** – breathing. Breath control related to the posture and movement in Kata.
- **Tyakugan** – the aiming points. In Kata you must keep the purpose of the movement in mind.
- **Kiai** – shouting. Shouting at set points in Kata to demonstrate the martial spirit.
- **Keitai No Hoji** – correct positioning. Correct positioning in movement and stance.
- **Zanshin** – remaining on guard. Remaining on guard at the completion of the Kata (i.e. back to "Yoi") until told to relax "Enoy".

TAIKYOKU SHODAN

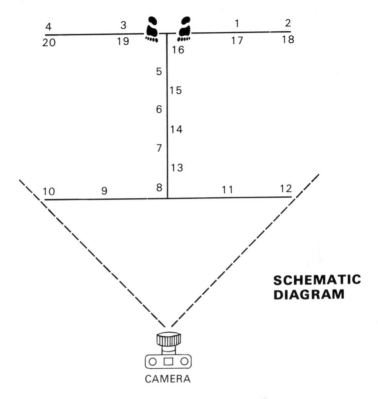

SCHEMATIC DIAGRAM

CAMERA

Of the three Taikyoku forms, Shōdan is the most elementary and consists of one block, one attack and one stance.

Once someone is able to perform the Taikyoku forms with proficiency, he can understand the other Kata with relative ease.

To quote Funakoshi: "Because of its simplicity the Kata is easily learned by beginners, nevertheless, as its name implies*, this form is of the most profound character and one to which, upon mastery of the art of Karate, an expert will return to select it as the ultimate training Kata".

* Taikyoku is a philosophical term denoting the macrocosm before its differentiation into heaven and earth: hence, chaos or the void.

Left: Hidari Gedan Barai

YOI

1

HIDARI GEDAN BARAI

3

MIGI GEDAN BARAI

4

HIDARI OI ZUKI

2

MIGI OI ZUKI

FAST

5

HIDARI GEDAN BARAI

FAST

FAST

6

MIGI OI ZUKI

7

HIDARI OI ZUKI

FAST

FAST

9

HIDARI GEDAN BARAI

10

MIGI OI ZUKI

FAST  KIAI

8

MIGI OI ZUKI

FAST

11

MIGI GEDAN BARAI

12

HIDARI OI ZUKI

13

HIDARI GEDAN BARAI

FAST

FAST KIAI

15

HIDARI OI ZUKI

16

MIGI OI ZUKI

FAST

14

MIGI OI ZUKI

FAST

17

HIDARI GEDAN BARAI

FAST   **FAST**

18   19

MIGI OI ZUKI   **MIGI GEDAN BARAI**

YAME

FAST

20

HIDARI OI ZUKI

13-16 FRONT VIEW

FAST

FAST

13

HIDARI GEDAN BARAI

14

MIGI OI ZUKI

FAST **KIAI**

16

MIGI OI ZUKI

110

FAST

15

HIDARI OI ZUKI

APPLICATIONS

A1

A2

B1

B2

C1

C2

TAIKYOKU SHODAN

A3

A4

B3

B4

B5

C3

C4

TAIKYOKU SHODAN

YOI

1

2

6

7

8 KIAI

12

13

14

18

19

20

3

4

5

9

10

11

15

16

KIAI

17

YAME

HEIAN SHODAN

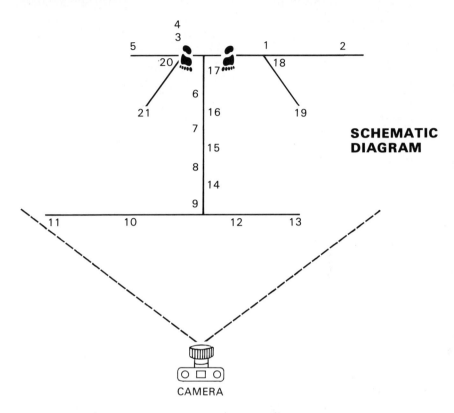

SCHEMATIC DIAGRAM

CAMERA

The word Heian means "Peaceful Mind", Heian Sho Dan being the first of five Heian Katas. It has 21 movements and takes about 40 seconds to perform.

Students should concentrate on perfecting the forward and back stances in this Kata. For the first time, Shutō Uke is introduced together with Age Uke and Tettsui Uchi. Sensei Itosu, the man credited with the compilation of the Heian Katas in the early 1900s set great store in the proficient execution of this Kata.

Left: Migi Jodan Age Uke

YOI

1
HIDARI GEDAN BARAI

3
MIGI GEDAN BARAI

4
MIGI TETTSUI UCHI

FAST

2
MIGI OI ZUKI

FAST

5
HIDARI OI ZUKI

FAST   **FAST**

6
HIDARI GEDAN BARAI

7
MIGI AGE UKE

FAST ⟨KIAI⟩   **FAST**

9
MIGI AGE UKE

10
HIDARI GEDAN BARAI

8
HIDARI AGE UKE

11
MIGI OI ZUKI

FAST

FAST

12
MIGI GEDAN BARAI

13
HIDARI OI ZUKI

FAST

FAST

15
MIGI OI ZUKI

16
HIDARI OI ZUKI

FAST

14

HIDARI GEDAN BARAI

FAST **KIAI**

17

MIGI OI ZUKI

FAST

FAST

18

HIDARI SHUTŌ UKE

19

MIGI SHUTŌ UKE

FAST

FAST

21

HIDARI SHUTŌ UKE

YAME

20
MIGI SHUTŌ UKE

MOVEMENTS 14·17

FAST

FAST

14

HIDARI GEDAN BARAI

15

MIGI OI ZUKI

FAST

KIAI

17

MIGI OI ZUKI

FRONT VIEW

FAST

16

HIDARI OI ZUKI

APPLICATIONS

A1

A2

A6

B1

C1

C2

C3

D1

D2

D3

HEIAN SHODAN

A3   A4   A5

B2   B3   B4

TAI SABAKI

C4

HEIAN SHODAN

YOI   1   2

6   7   8

12   13   14

18   19   20

130

YAME

HEIAN NIDAN

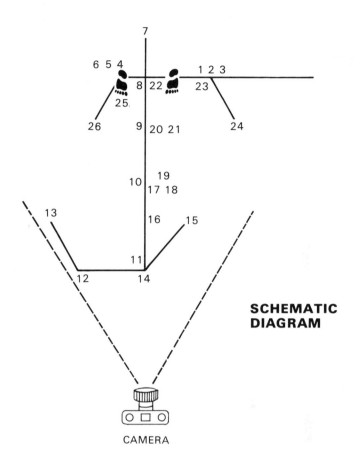

SCHEMATIC DIAGRAM

CAMERA

Heian Nidan carries on where Heian Shodan left off. Having learned the back stance, it is now used to open the Kata and performs in conjunction with Haiwan-Jōdan-Uke. We also see the arrival of techniques like Ura Zuki, Uraken Uchi, Shihon Nukite, and kicking techniques begin to appear in the form of Mae Geri and Yoko Geri. An interesting point concerns the change of direction when executing Yoko Geri Keage.

This Kata requires about 40 seconds to complete the 26 movements.

Left: Migi Chūdan Shihon Nukite

133

YOI

1

HIDARI JŌDAN HAIWAN UKE

3

HIDARI CHŪDAN ZUKI

4

MIGI JŌDAN HAIWAN UKE

FAST

2

MIGI URA ZUKI

FAST

5

HIDARI URA ZUKI

FAST

FAST

6

MIGI CHŪDAN ZUKI

7

YOKO KEAGE-URAKEN

FAST

FAST

9

MIGI SHUTŌ UKE

10

HIDARI SHUTŌ UKE

FAST

8

HIDARI SHUTŌ UKE

FAST  **KIAI**

11

MIGI CHUDAN SHIHON
NUKITE – KIAI

FAST

FAST

12

HIDARI SHUTŌ UKE

13

MIGI SHUTŌ UKE

FAST

FAST

15

HIDARI SHUTŌ UKE

16

**MIGI
UCHI UKE**　**GYAKU
HANMI**

FAST

14

MIGI SHUTŌ UKE

FAST

17

MIGI
MAE GERI

139

FAST

FAST

18

**HIDARI CHŪDAN
GYAKU ZUKI**

19

**HIDARI CHŪDAN
UCHI UKE
GYAKU HANMI**

FAST

FAST

21

**MIGI CHŪDAN
GYAKU ZUKI**

22

**MIGI CHŪDAN
MOROTE UKE**

FAST

20

HIDARI MAE GERI

FAST

23

HIDARI
GEDAN BARAI

141

24

MIGI AGE UKE

25

MIGI GEDAN BARAI

YAME

26

HIDARI AGE UKE KIAI

15-16 FRONT VIEW

A   **B**   **C**   **D**

17-22 FRONT VIEW

FAST

FAST

17

MIGI MAE GERI

18

HIDARI GYAKU ZUKI

FAST

FAST

20

HIDARI MAE GERI

21

MIGI GYAKU ZUKI

FAST

19

HIDARI UCHI UKE

FAST

22

MIGI MOROTE UKE

145

APPLICATIONS

HEIAN NIDAN

HEIAN NIDAN

YOI

1

2

6

7

8

12

13

14

18

19

20

24

25

26

KIAI

3

4

5

9

KIAI

11

15

16

17

21

22

23

YAME

HEIAN SANDAN

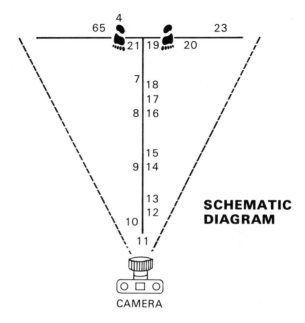

SCHEMATIC DIAGRAM

CAMERA

Heian Sandan begins with Chudan Uchi Uke again performed in Kokutsu Dachi and is followed by Kosa Uke, which in my opinion has been introduced perhaps a little prematurely. Using Kōsa Uke to Block either a Mae Geri or an Oi Zuki is fair enough, despite the degree of difficulty in synchronisation and harmony, however, blocking Yama Zuki is a different kettle of fish and requires much practise together with an ability to "Kime" and relax speedily, ready for the next attack and corresponding Kōsa Uke.

For the first time in Kata, we see the appearance of Fumikomi and Empi Uke and the simultaneous attack of Ushiro Empi and Tate Zuki.

The 21 movements should take 40 seconds to complete.

Left: Hidari Tate Zuki – Migi Empi

YOI

1

HIDARI CHŪDAN UCHI UKE

3

KŌSA UKE

4

MIGI CHŪDAN UCHI UKE

152

2

KŌSA UKE

FAST

5

KŌSA UKE

6

KŌSA UKE

7

HIDARI MOROTE UKE

9

HIDARI TETTSUI UCHI

10

MIGI CHŪDAN OI ZUKI

8

MIGI SHIHON NUKITE

SLOW

11

**RYOKEN
KOSHI GAMAE**

FAST

FAST

12

MIGI EMPI UKE

13

JŌDAN URAKEN UCHI

FAST

FAST

15

HIDARI URAKEN UCHI

16

MIGI EMPI UKE

14

HIDARI EMPI UKE

17

MIGI URAKEN UCHI

157

SLOW   **FAST**

18
**MIGI CHŪDAN TATE
SHUTO UKE**

19
**HIDARI CHŪDAN
OI ZUKI**

FAST  **KIAI**

21
**HIDARI TATE ZUKI
MIGI EMPI**

YAME

20

**MIGI TATE ZUKI
HIDARI EMPI**

19-20 FRONT VIEW

19

**HIDARI CHŪDAN
OI ZUKI**

20

**MIGI TATE ZUKI
HIDARI EMPI**

11-19 FRONT VIEW

SLOW

11

**RYOKEN KOSHI
GAMAE**

FAST

12

MIGI EMPI UKE

FAST

14

HIDARI EMPI UKE

FAST

15

HIDARI URAKEN UCHI

FAST

17

MIGI URAKEN UCHI

SLOW

18

**MIGI CHŪDAN TATE
SHUTO UKE**

160

FAST

13

JŌDAN URAKEN UCHI

FAST

16

MIGI EMPI UCHI

FAST

19

**HIDARI CHŪDAN
OI ZUKI**

APPLICATIONS

A1 A2 A3

B1 B2 B3

B7 D1

C1 C2 C3

HEIAN SANDAN

A4

A5

A6

B4

B5

B6

D2

D3

C4

HEIAN SANDAN

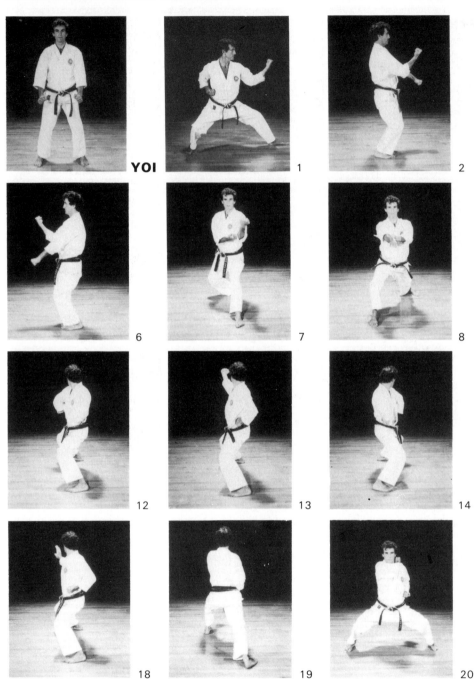

YOI 1 2

6 7 8

12 13 14

18 19 20

164

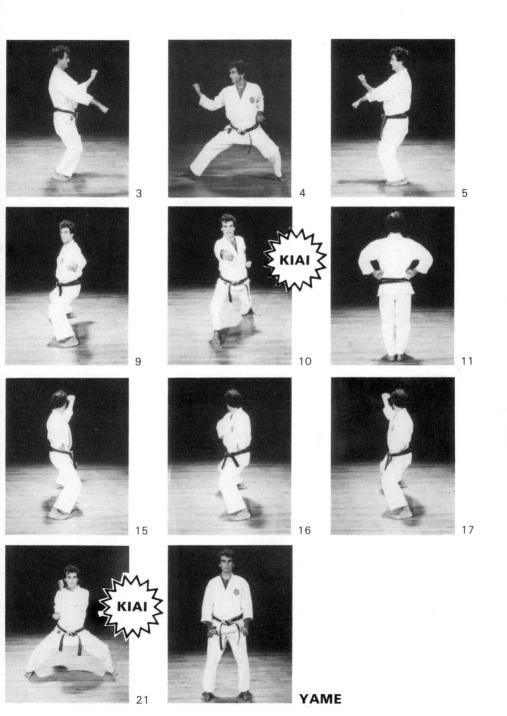

3

4

5

KIAI

9

10

11

15

16

17

KIAI

21

YAME

HEIAN YONDAN

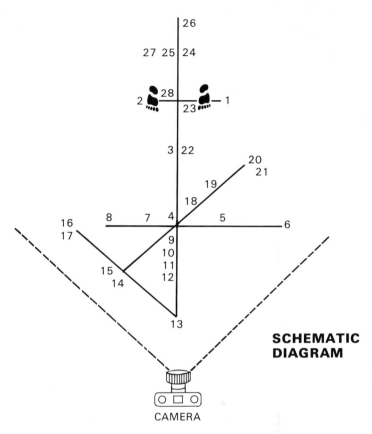

SCHEMATIC DIAGRAM

CAMERA

Heian Yondan provides the most variation of any Heian Kata and with it, the awareness of the vast number of techniques to be mastered in the future.

Beginning with Haishu Haiwan Uke one learns to harmonise the arms together, develop the power in the block by augmenting one arm with the other, giving the student the opportunity to develop "kime" " through dynamic tension. Appearing for the first time are Juji Uke, Gedan Shutō, Shutō Uchi, Kakiwake Uke and Hiza Geri.

When performing Hiza Geri, equal concentration and power distribution must take place when attacking with the right knee and pulling the head down onto it with both hands. It is important to contract the Hara and use to the optimum the muscles at the side of the body. (Latissimus Dorsi).

Left: Migi Jodan Mae Geri

YOI

1

HAISHU HAIWAN UKE

FAST

FAST

3

GEDAN JUJI UKE

4

MIGI CHŪDAN
MOROTE UKE

2

HAISHU HAIWAN UKE

FAST

5

**YOKO KEAGE
URAKEN
UCHI**

FAST

FAST

6

MIGI MAE EMPI

7

YOKO KEAGE
URAKEN UCHI

FAST

FAST

9

HIDARI GEDAN
SHUTŌ BARAI

10

MIGI JŌDAN
SHUTŌ UCHI

FAST

8

HIDARI MAE EMPI

FAST

11

**MIGI JŌDAN
MAE GERI**

11–12–13 ARE ALL ONE MOVEMENT BUT SHOWN HERE SEPARATELY TO AVOID CONFUSION

FAST

FAST **KIAI**

12

HIDARI TEISHO UKE

13

MIGI CHŪDAN URAKEN UCHI

FAST

FAST

16

MIGI CHŪDAN OI ZUKI

MIGI JŌDAN MAE GERI

172

14

CHŪDAN KAKIWAKE UKE

FAST

17

HIDARI CHŪDAN
GYAKU ZUKI

173

FAST

18

**CHŪDAN KAKIWAKE
UKE**

19

**HIDARI JŌDAN MAE
GERI**

FAST

FAST

21

**MIGI CHŪDAN
GYAKU ZUKI**

22

**HIDARI CHUDAN
MOROTE UKE**

FAST

20

**HIDARI CHŪDAN
OI ZUKI**

FAST

23

**MIGI CHŪDAN
MOROTE UKE**

24

**HIDARI CHŪDAN
MOROTE UKE**

25

MOROTE KUBI OSAE

27

**HIDARI CHŪDAN
SHUTŌ UKE**

28

**MIGI CHŪDAN
SHUTŌ UKE**

26

MIGI HIZA GERI UCHI

YAME

21-26 FRONT VIEW

FAST

FAST

21

MIGI CHŪDAN GYAKU ZUKI

22

HIDARI CHŪDAN MOROTE UKE

FAST

FAST

24

HIDARI CHŪDAN MOROTE UKE

25

MOROTE KUBI OSAE

FAST

23

**MIGI CHŪDAN
MOROTE UKE**

FAST

KIAI

26

**MIGI HIZA
GERI UCHI**

APPLICATIONS

BLOCKING

GRABBING

STRIKING

A1

A2

A3

BLOCKING

STRIKING

B4

B5

KICKING

C1

PUNCHING

PUNCHING

D3

D4

BLOCKING

E1

HEIAN YONDAN

BLOCKING
BLOCKING & STRIKING
KICKING

B1   B2   B3

STRIKING
GRABBING
KICKING

C2   D1   D2

GRABBING
KICKING

E2   E3

HEIAN YONDAN

YOI

1

2

6

7

8

12

13 KIAI

14

18

19

20

24

25

26 KIAI

3

4

5

9

10

11

15

16

17

21

22

23

27

28

YAME

HEIAN GŌDAN

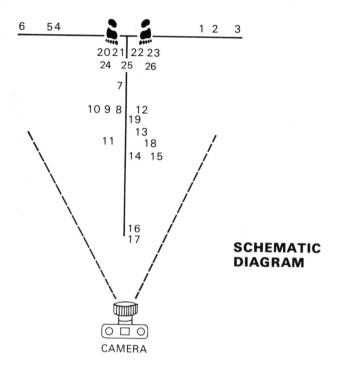

6   54   1 2 3

20 21 | 22 23
24 25   26

7

10 9 8 | 12
19
13
11   18
14 15

16
17

SCHEMATIC DIAGRAM

CAMERA

Heian Go Dan introduces the student to many new techniques, none more important than Mizuno-Nagare-No-Kamae – The Flowing Water Technique. This technique is of course for punching but has spiritual connotations. The Forearm, although parallel to the chest, should be inclined slightly downwards with the feeling of water flowing down the arm from the shoulder.

For the first time we see Jōdan Haishu Juji Uke, Morote Tsuki Age and Gedan Nukite.

Jumping over a "Bo" attack to avoid having the legs broken provides an adequate and new experience in Karate movements.

There are 26 movements and they should occupy about 50 seconds.

Left: Migi Mikazuki Geri

YOI

1
HIDARI CHŪDAN UCHI UKE

**LONG INHALATION
SLOW**

3
HIDARI KAGI GAMAE

FAST

4
MIGI CHŪDAN UCHI UKE

186

2

**MIGI CHŪDAN
GYAKU ZUKI**

5

**HIDARI CHŪDAN
GYAKU ZUKI**

187

LONG INHALATION
SLOW

FAST

6

MIGI KAGI GAMAE

7

**MIGI CHŪDAN
MOROTE UKE**

FAST

FAST

9

**JODAN HAISHU
JUJI UKE**

10

CHŪDAN OSAE UKE

188

FAST

8

GEDAN JUJI UKE

FAST **KIAI**

11

**CHŪDAN MIGI
OI ZUKI**

189

12

MIGI GEDAN BARAI

13

CHŪDAN HAISHU UKE

FAST

FAST

15

MIGI MAE EMPI

16

**MIGI CHŪDAN
MOROTE UKE**

FAST

14

MIGI MIKAZUKI GERI

FAST

17

KŌHŌ TSUKI
AGE

KIAI

18

JUMPING OVER BO

19

GEDAN JŪJI UKE

21

**MIGI GEDAN
SHUTŌ UCHI**

22

**MANJI GAMAE
IN KŌKUTSU DACHI**

FAST

20

**MIGI CHŪDAN
MOROTE UKE**

LONG INHALATION
SLOW

23

**MANJI GAMAE
IN HEISOKU DACHI**

FAST

FAST

24

**MANJI GAMAE
IN HEISOKU DACHI**

25

**HIDARI GEDAN
SHUTŌ UCHI**

27

YAME

FAST

26

MANJI GAMAE
IN KŌKUTSU DACHI

19-20 FRONT VIEW

FAST

FAST

GEDAN JUJI UKE

MIGI CHŪDAN
MOROTE UKE

11-12 SIDE VIEW

FAST

FAST

KIAI

CHŪDAN MIGI OI ZUKI

MIGI GEDAN BARAI

196

APPLICATIONS

YOI

BLOCKING

PUNCHING

A1

A2

A3

BLOCKING A KICK

BLOCKING A PUNCH

BLOCKING A PUNCH

B1

B2

B3

PUSHING BACK

PUNCHING

B4

B5

197

APPLICATIONS

READY TO ATTACK — C1

BLOCKING — C2

BLOCKING — C3

E1

BLOCKING — E2

PUNCHING — E3

BLOCKING — G1

BLOCKING & STRIKING — G2

GRABBING — G3

HEIAN GODAN

BLOCKING

D1

KICKING

D2

STRIKING

D3

JUMPING OVER BO

F1

F2

F3

BLOCKING

F4

BREAKING GRIP

G4

HEIAN GODAN

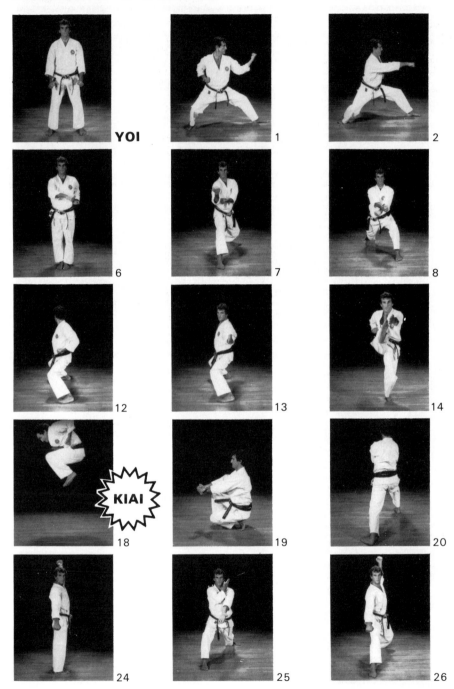

YOI   1   2

6   7   8

12   13   14

KIAI   18   19   20

24   25   26

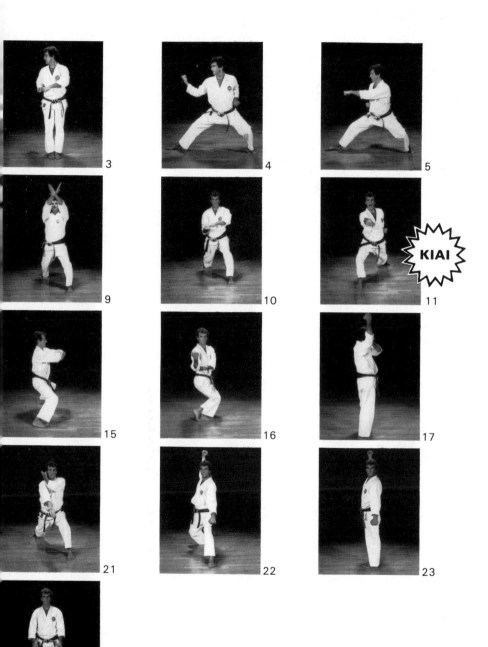

KIAI

YAME

PART 3 KUMITE
SPARRING

The following pages show the step-by-step method of learning the various types of Kumite that eventually lead up to Jiyu Kumite (Free Style Sparring).

Each of the three, Go Hon Kumite, Sambon Kumite and Kihon Ippon Kumite are of great importance if the Karateka wishes to become proficient in Jiyu Kumite.

Today, more and more people are being attracted to Karate for what I consider the wrong reasons. Let me put it another way – people are being attracted to the Sport not the Art.

A contest should be about neither winning nor losing but participation. Many people enter competitions today for the wrong reasons.

Tournaments bring out a person's ego quite often and that person loves to hear the roar of the crowd, wants to receive a big cash prize or silver trophy, and on occasions like this – it's hard to spot humility, or the many other attributes the Martial Art inspires.

Karate is a fighting art and Kumite is an intrinsic part of it. Jiyu Kumite is a part of overall Karate training, but let's keep things in perspective – it's just a part – and no more.

The moment a Gyaku Zuki scores

GO HON KUMITE
5 ATTACK SPARRING

Go Hon Kumite is the first Kumite practise in Shotokan. It consists of five attacks (stepping), five defences and a counter attack.

Go Hon Kumite is designed to develop strong attacks and strong blocks and teach control on the counter attack.

It also helps the beginner begin to appreciate such factors as timing, distancing and breathing.

Up until this time in basic training, the student has only performed his techniques in mid air, now he has a face or stomach to aim at, and this helps from the point of view of accuracy.

Finally, all the techniques are pre-arranged and there is one Kiai on the counter attack.

Left: Hidari Jōdan Age Uke

No. 1 JŌDAN

TRAINING METHOD FOR GO HON KUMITE (WITHOUT PARTNER)

STEPPING →

START

| YOI | GEDAN BARAI | OI ZUKI | OI ZUKI |

**FROM YOI STEP BACK
INTO GEDAN BARAI**

← STEPPING BACK

FINISH

| YOI | RIGHT GYAKU ZUKI | AGE UKE | AGE UKE |

**AFTER GYAKU ZUKI
STEP BACK INTO
YOI POSITION**

FORWARD

OI ZUKI	OI ZUKI	OI ZUKI	YOI

AFTER 5TH OI ZUKI STEP FORWARD INTO YOI POSITION

STEPPING BACK

AGE UKE	AGE UKE	AGE UKE	YOI

No. 2 CHŪDAN

TRAINING METHOD FOR GO HON KUMITE (WITHOUT PARTNER)

STEPPING →

START

| YOI | GEDAN BARAI | OI ZUKI | OI ZUKI |

FROM YOI STEP BACK
INTO GEDAN BARAI

← STEPPING

FINISH

| YOI | GYAKU ZUKI | SOTO UKE | SOTO UKE |

AFTER GYAKU ZUKI
STEP BACK INTO
YOI POSITION

FINISH

OI ZUKI　　　**OI ZUKI**　　　**OI ZUKI**　　　**YOI**

**AFTER 5TH ZUKI
STEP FORWARD INTO
YOI POSITION**

BACK

START

SOTO UKE　　　**SOTO UKE**　　　**SOTO UKE**　　　**YOI**

No. 3 MAE GERI
TRAINING METHOD FOR GO HON KUMITE (WITHOUT PARTNER)

STEPPING →

START

YOI   FORWARD STANCE   MAE GERI   MAE GERI

FROM YOI STEP
BACK INTO
ZENKUTSU DACHI

← **STEPPING**

FINISH

YOI   GYAKU ZUKI   GEDAN BARAI   GEDAN BARAI

AFTER GYAKU ZUKI
STEP BACK INTO
YOI POSITION

FINISH

| MAE GERI | MAE GERI | MAE GERI | YOI |

**STEP FORWARD
INTO YOI POSITION**

BACK

START

| GEDAN BARAI | GEDAN BARAI | GEDAN BARAI | YOI |

**FROM YOI POSITION
STEP BACK**

GO HON KUMITE

YOI

ATTACKER STEPS BACK
GEDAN BARAI

MIGI 3 HIDARI
OI ZUKI AGE UKE

HIDARI 4 MIGI
OI ZUKI AGE UKE

JŌDAN ATTACK

MIGI OI ZUKI	1	HIDARI AGE UKE

HIDARI OI ZUKI	2	MIGI AGE UKE

MIGI OI ZUKI	5	HIDARI AGE UKE

COUNTER ATTACK RIGHT GYAKU ZUKI (KIAI)

AFTER, BOTH MOVE IN THIS DIRECTION ⟶

GO HON KUMITE

YOI

**ATTACKER STEPS BACK
GEDAN BARAI**

**MIGI
OI ZUKI**   3   **HIDARI
SOTO UDE UKE**

**HIDARI
OI ZUKI**   4   **MIGI SOTO
UDE UKE**

CHŪDAN ATTACK

| MIGI | 1 | HIDARI |
| OI ZUKI | | SOTO UDE UKE |

| MIGI | 2 | MIGI SOTO |
| OI ZUKI | | UDE UKE |

| MIGI | 5 | HIDARI |
| OI ZUKI | | SOTO UDE UKE |

COUNTER ATTACK
CHUDAN GYAKU ZUKI (KIAI)

AFTER, BOTH MOVE IN THIS
DIRECTION ⟶

GO HON KUMITE

YOI

ATTACKER STEPS BACK
IN ZENKUTSU DACHI

MIGI   3   HIDARI
MAE GERI   GEDAN BARAI

HIDARI   4   MIGI
MAE GERI   GEDAN BARAI

MAE GERI ATTACK

MIGI MAE GERI 1 **HIDARI GEDAN BARAI**

HIDARI MAE GERI 2 **MIGI GEDAN BARAI**

MIGI MAE GERI 5 **HIDARI GEDAN BARAI**

COUNTER ATTACK WITH RIGHT GYAKU ZUKI

AFTER, BOTH MOVE IN THIS DIRECTION ⟶

217

SAMBON KUMITE
3 LEVEL ATTACK SPARRING

Sambon Kumite or three-attack sparring can be performed in the same way as Go Hon Kumite, with the resulting benefits of developing strong blocks and attacks, together with improvement in "Kime".

On the other hand, Sambon Kumite may take the form of a multi-level sequence so providing pre arranged variation in attack and defence.

On the following pages, the reader will see this form demonstrated in the simple form of Jōdan Oi Zuki, Chūdan Oi Zuki and Chūdan Mae Geri attacks being countered with Age Uke, Soto Ude Uke, Mae Geri and Gyaku Zuki.

Once this simple routine has been perfected, there are no end to the number of hand and foot combinations that can be utilised.

As no attack and defence is usually repeated twice, Sambon Kumite prepares the students' mind for change and encourages him to think quickly.

Shortly he will advance to Kihon Ippon Kumite and its multitude of contrasting techniques, however – firstly he *must* master Sambon Kumite.

Left: Hidari Chūdan Soto Ude Uke

TRAINING METHOD FOR SAMBON KUMITE (WITHOUT PARTNER)

START

**FROM YOI ATTACKER STEPS
BACK INTO GEDAN BARAI**

1

FINISH

**STEP BACK INTO
YAME POSITION**

FINISH

2 **STEP FORWARD** 3
INTO YAME POSITION

START

**FROM YOI POSITION
STEP BACK**

SAMBON KUMITE

YOI

ATTACKER STEPS BACK
GEDAN BARAI

MAE GERI   3   HIDARI
CHŪDAN   GEDAN BARAI

COUNTER ATTACK
GYAKU ZUKI CHŪDAN

AFTER, BOTH MOVE IN THIS
DIRECTION ⟶

3 LEVEL ATTACK SPARRING

| OI ZUKI | 1 | HIDARI | OI ZUKI | 2 | MIGI SOTO |
| JŌDAN | | AGE UKE | CHŪDAN | | UDE UKE |

YAME

KIHON IPPON KUMITE
BASIC ONE ATTACK SPARRING

Sometimes called the Basic Kata of Sparring, Kihon Ippon Kumite, or basic 1-attack sparring, allows both persons to take it in turn attacking with pre-arranged techniques and defending and counter attacking.

One learns about "Maai" (Distancing) very early on and the fact that it is not necessary always to defend in straight lines. It is possible to move in other directions and parry the attacker rather than use brute force. Consequently, side stepping and moving at 45° lend themselves admirably for this purpose.

Kihon Ippon Kumite begins with the attacker in Gedan Barai and the defender in the Yoi position. The person defending having completed his counter attack with Kiai, then returns to the Yoi position. He does not pull into the free style "Kamae" pose in any circumstances.

Kihon Ippon Kumite is the formal exercise of sparring and should not be confused with Jiyu Ippon Kumite (semi free 1 attack sparring).

The attacker should attack strongly at all times, exercising control to the face but making some contact if possible when attacking to the mid section.

The defender, after blocking, should focus his counter attack just short of the target and on no account follow through and make contact.

When training in basics in a class situation we always step FORWARD into Gedan Barai. This is to show martial spirit. However, when training with a partner, as in Kihon Ippon Kumite, we always step BACK into Gedan Barai, thus showing humility and gratitude for having someone to train with.

Bowing ("Rei") before training together and after, signifies mutual respect.

Left: Jōdan Shuto Uchi

225

JŌDAN ATTACKS No. 1

SHIZENTAI   1   HIDARI GEDAN BARAI

HIDARI JŌDAN AGE UKE   3   MIGI JŌDAN OI ZUKI

HIDARI JŌDAN AGE UKE 2 **MIGI JŌDAN OI ZUKI**
(HALFWAY) **(HALFWAY)**

MIGI CHŪDAN GYAKU ZUKI 4 **MIGI JŌDAN OI ZUKI**

JŌDAN No. 2

SHIZENTAI   1   **HIDARI GEDAN BARAI**

HIDARI JŌDAN TATE SHUTŌ UKE   3   **MIGI JŌDAN OI ZUKI**

HIDARI JŌDAN TATE SHUTŌ UKE 2 **MIGI JŌDAN OI ZUKI**
(HALFWAY)   **(HALFWAY)**

MIGI JŌDAN SHUTŌ UCHI   4   **MIGI JŌDAN OI ZUKI**

JŌDAN No. 3

SHIZENTAI   1   **HIDARI GEDAN BARAI**

MIGI YOKO GERI KEAGE   3   **MIGI JŌDAN OI ZUKI**

MIGI JŌDAN AGE UKE   2   **MIGI JŌDAN OI ZUKI**
IN HEISOKU DACHI

MIGI CHŪDAN YOKO EMPI   4   **MIGI JŌDAN OI ZUKI**

JŌDAN No. 4

SHIZENTAI　　1　　HIDARI GEDAN BARAI

MIGI CHŪDAN MAWASHI GERI　　3　　MIGI JŌDAN OI ZUKI

232

HAISHU JŪJI UKE   2   **MIGI JŌDAN OI ZUKI**

HIDARI USHIRO MAWASHI EMPI 4   **MIGI JŌDAN OI ZUKI**

CHŪDAN ATTACKS No. 1

SHIZENTAI   1   **HIDARI GEDAN BARAI**

HIDARI CHŪDAN SOTO UDE UKE   3   **MIGI CHŪDAN OI ZUKI**

HIDARI CHŪDAN SOTO UDE UKE 2   **MIGI CHŪDAN OI ZUKI**
(HALFWAY)   **(HALFWAY)**

MIGI CHŪDAN GYAKU ZUKI   4   **MIGI CHŪDAN OI ZUKI**

235

CHŪDAN No. 2

SHIZENTAI 1 **HIDARI GEDAN BARAI**

MIGI CHŪDAN SOTO UDE UKE 3 **MIGI CHŪDAN OI ZUKI**

MIGI CHŪDAN SOTO UDE UKE 2 **MIGI CHŪDAN OI ZUKI**
(HALFWAY) **(HALFWAY)**

MIGI CHŪDAN YOKO EMPI 4 **MIGI CHŪDAN OI ZUKI**

CHŪDAN No. 3

SHIZENTAI   1   **HIDARI GEDAN BARAI**

HIDARI JŌDAN KIZAMI ZUKI   3   **MIGI CHŪDAN OI ZUKI**

HIDARI CHŪDAN UCHI UDE UKE 2   **MIGI CHŪDAN OI ZUKI**

MIGI CHŪDAN GYAKU ZUKI 4   **MIGI CHŪDAN OI ZUKI**

CHŪDAN No. 4

SHIZENTAI 1 **HIDARI GEDAN BARAI**

HIDARI CHŪDAN KIZAMI MAE GERI 3 **MIGI CHŪDAN OI ZUKI**

HIDARI CHŪDAN SHUTO UKE 2 **MIGI CHŪDAN OI ZUKI**

MIGI CHŪDAN NUKITE 4 **MIGI CHŪDAN OI ZUKI**

241

MAE GERI ATTACKS No. 1

SHIZENTAI 1 **HIDARI ZENKUTSU DACHI**

HIDARI GEDAN BARAI 3 **MIGI CHŪDAN MAE GERI**

HIDARI GEDAN BARAI 2 **MIGI CHŪDAN MAE GERI**
(HALFWAY) **(HALFWAY)**

MIGI CHŪDAN GYAKU ZUKI 4 **MIGI ZENKUTSU DACHI**

MAE GERI No. 2

SHIZENTAI   1   **HIDARI ZENKUTSU DACHI**

HIDARI JŌDAN KIZAMI ZUKI   3

MIGI GEDAN BARAI 2 **MIGI CHŪDAN MAE GERI**
GYAKU HANMI

MIGI CHŪDAN GYAKU ZUKI 4 **MIGI ZENKUTSU DACHI**

245

MAE GERI No. 3

SHIZENTAI   1   **HIDARI ZENKUTSU DACHI**

PULLING BACK   3   **MIGI ZENKUTSU DACHI**
(HALFWAY POINT)

GEDAN JŪJI UKE   2   **MIGI CHŪDAN MAE GERI**

JŌDAN SHUTŌ JUJI UKE   4   **MIGI ZENKUTSU DACHI**
(A BLOCK USED AS AN ATTACK)

MAE GERI No. 4

SHIZENTAI   1   HIDARI ZENKUTSU DACHI

HIDARI CHŪDAN TATE SHUTŌ UKE 3   MIGI CHŪDAN
MIGI NEKO ASHI DACHI   MAE GERI SNAPPING BACK

MIGI GEDAN BARAI   2   **MIGI CHŪDAN MAE GERI**
MIGI NEKO ASHI DACHI

MIGI CHŪDAN MAE EMPI   4

YOKO GERI KEKOMI ATTACKS No.

SHIZENTAI   1   HIDARI ZENKUTSU DACHI

HIDARI CHŪDAN SOTO   3   MIGI CHŪDAN YOKI
UDE UKE   GERI KEKOMI

HIDARI CHŪDAN SOTO UDE UKE (HALFWAY) 2 **MIGI CHŪDAN YOKO GERI KEKOMI (HALFWAY)**

MIGI CHŪDAN GYAKU ZUKI 4

KEKOMI No. 2

SHIZENTAI   1   **HIDARI ZENKUTSU DACHI**

HIDARI GEDAN KAKE UKE   3   **MIGI CHŪDAN YOKO GERI KEKOMI**

HIDARI GEDAN KAKE UKE   2   **MIGI CHŪDAN YOKO**
(HALFWAY)   **GERI KEKOMI (HALFWAY)**

MIGI JŌDAN HAITO UCHI   4

MAWASHI GERI ATTACKS No. 1

1   HIDARI ZENKUTSU DACHI

HIDARI JŌDAN UCHI UDE UKE   3   MIGI JŌDAN MAWASHI GERI

HIDARI JŌDAN UCHI UDE UKE 2 **MIGI JŌDAN MAWASHI GERI**
(HALFWAY) **(HALFWAY)**

MIGI CHŪDAN GYAKU ZUKI 4

MAWASHI GERI No. 2

1   **HIDARI ZENKUTSU DACHI**

MIGI JŌDAN MAWASHI GERI   3   **JŌDAN SHUTŌ MOROTE UKE**

JŌDAN SHUTŌ MOROTE UKE 2 **MIGI JŌDAN MAWASHI GERI**
(HALFWAY) **(HALFWAY)**

MIGI CHŪDAN MOROTE YOKO EMPI 4

KIHON IPPON KUMITE. SET 5

Set 5 consists of 5 attacks. One Jōdan Oi Zuki, one Chūdan Oi Zuki, one Chūdan Mae Geri, one Chūdan Yoko Geri Kekomi and one Jōdan Mawashi Geri, together with five designated defences and counter attacks.

DEFENCES

JŌDAN ATTACK No. 5 DEFENCE

SHIZENTAI/ NATURAL STANCE.	HIDARI GEDAN BARAI/ LEFT DOWNWARD BLOCK (FORWARD STANCE).	HIDARI JŌDAN AGE UKE/ LEFT UPPER RISING BLOCK (FORWARD STANCE).	MIGI JŌDAN OI ZUKI/ RIGHT UPPER STEPPING PUNCH (FORWARD STANCE).

CHŪDAN ATTACK No. 5 DEFENCE

SHIZENTAI/ NATURAL STANCE.	HIDARI GEDAN BARAI/ LEFT DOWNWARD BLOCK (FORWARD STANCE).	HIDARI CHŪDAN EMPI UKE/ LEFT MIDDLE ELBOW BLOCK (STRADDLE STANCE).	MIGI CHŪDAN OI ZUKI RIGHT MIDDLE STEPPING PUNCH (FORWARD STANCE).

Originally, the Beginners Guide to Shotokan Karate was produced as a working manual to assist the student in the fundamentals of the style, as taught by his own instructor. Almost a decade later it has become **The Beginners Text Book** and is sold in most English speaking countries and surprisingly enough, in Japan too.
Omitted in previous editions but now included is Kihon Ippon Kumite Set 5. This is the last *formal* set in Shotokan but numerous other techniques of Kihon Ippon Kumite are practised on an individual basis.
As the student approaches Set 5, his understanding of *Sabaki* (Stepping and Dodging) should have improved. Techniques should now be performed correctly, with good posture and proper breathing. *Zanshin* (Awareness) should be keener and *Yomi* (Perceptivity) playing an almost intuitive role.
Throughout the practice of Kihon Ippon Kumite, Sahō (Etiquette) should prevail, despite the students degree of tiredness. Finally, as with previous Kumite, briefly maintain the focus (Kime) of the final counter attack. This will enable the correct muscles to be tensed and developed accordingly.

BEFORE MAE GERI, PULL LEFT FOOT BACK 1/2 STEP FOR CORRECT DISTANCING.

| MIGI JŌDAN MAE GERI/ RIGHT UPPER FRONT KICK. | MIGI JŌDAN OI ZUKI/ RIGHT UPPER STEPPING PUNCH (FORWARD STANCE). | MIGI TATE EMPI UCHI/ RIGHT (VERTICAL) UPPER RISING ELBOW STRIKE (FORWARD STANCE). | MIGI JŌDAN OI ZUKI/ RIGHT UPPER STEPPING PUNCH (FORWARD STANCE). |

| HALF-WAY POSITION TO USHIRO MAWASHI EMPI UCHI. | | MIGI JŌDAN USHIRO MAWASHI EMPI UCHI/ RIGHT UPPER REVERSE (BACK) ROUNDHOUSE ELBOW STRIKE (STRADDLE STANCE). | MIGI CHŪDAN OI ZUKI/ RIGHT MIDDLE STEPPING PUNCH (FORWARD STANCE). |

MAE GERI ATTACK No. 5 DEFENCE

SHIZENTAI/ NATURAL STANCE.	HIDARI ZENKUTSU DACHI/ LEFT FORWARD STANCE.	HALFWAY POSITION TO HIDARI SUKUI UKE.

YOKO GERI KEKOMI ATTACK No. 3 DEFENCE

SHIZENTAI/ NATURAL STANCE.	HIDARI ZENKUTSU DACHI/ LEFT FORWARD STANCE.	MIGI USHIRO GEDAN BARAI/ RIGHT BACK DOWNWARD BLOCK IN FORWARD STANCE.	MIGI CHŪDAN YOKO GERI KEKOMI/ RIGHT MIDDLE SIDE THRUST KICK.

MAWASHI GERI ATTACK No. 3 DEFENCE

SHIZENTAI/ NATURAL STANCE.	HIDARI ZENKUTSU DACHI/ LEFT FORWARD STANCE	MIGI JŌDAN SOTO UDE UKE IN KIBA DACHI/ RIGHT UPPER OUTSIDE FOREARM BLOCK IN STRADDLE STANCE.	MIGI JŌDAN MAWASHI GERI/ RIGHT UPPER ROUNDHOUSE KICK

LIDARI SUKUI UKE IN KŌKUTSU DACHI/ LEFT SCOOPING BLOCK IN BACK STANCE

MIGI CHUDAN MAE GERI/ RIGHT MIDDLE FRONT KICK

MIGI CHŪDAN GYAKU ZUKI/ RIGHT MIDDLE REVERSE PUNCH IN FORWARD STANCE

MIGI ZENKUTSU DACHI/ RIGHT FORWARD STANCE

MIGI CHŪDAN YOKO GERI KEKOMI/ RIGHT MIDDLE SIDE THRUST KICK.

MIGI ZENKUTSU DACHI/ RIGHT FORWARD STANCE.

MIGI CHŪDAN YOKO EMPI UCHI IN KIBA DACHI/ RIGHT MIDDLE SIDE ELBOW STRIKE IN STRADDLE STANCE.

MIGI ZENKUTSU DACHI/ RIGHT FORWARD STANCE.

MIGI CHŪDAN MAE KIZAMI GERI/ RIGHT MIDDLE FRONT LEG SNAPPING KICK.

MIGI ZENKUTSU DACHI/ RIGHT FORWARD STANCE.

HIDARI CHŪDAN GYAKU ZUKI/ LEFT MIDDLE REVERSE PUNCH IN FORWARD STANCE.

MIGI ZENKUTSU DACHI/ RIGHT FORWARD STANCE.

261

TASK GRADE ORDER AND BELT SYSTEM

Grade	Colour of Belt
Beginner	White Belt
10th Kyu	Blue Belt
9th Kyu	Red Belt
8th Kyu	Orange Belt
7th Kyu Intermediate	Orange with Yellow Stripe
7th Kyu	Yellow Belt
6th Kyu Intermediate	Yellow with Green Stripe
6th Kyu	Green Belt
5th Kyu Intermediate	Green with Purple Stripe
5th Kyu	Purple Belt
4th Kyu Intermediate	Purple with 1 White Stripe
4th Kyu	Purple with 2 White Stripes
3rd Kyu Intermediate	Purple with 1 Brown Stripe
3rd Kyu	Brown Belt
2nd Kyu Intermediate	Brown with 1 White Stripe
2nd Kyu	Brown with 2 White Stripes
1st Kyu Intermediate	Brown with 1 Red Stripe
1st Kyu	Brown with 2 Red Stripes
1st Dan Intermediate	Brown with 1 Black Stripe
1st Dan	Black Belt

The eight intermediate grades are for juniors under 14 years.

The intermediate grade syllabus is the same as the next higher grade.

All grades given and ratified by T.A.S.K. are officially recognised by The Martial Arts Commission and the World Union of Karate Organisations.

T.A.S.K. Chief Instructor and Examiner: Sensei J. van Weenen, 6th Dan.

10th KYU – BLUE BELT

Basics

Technique	Stance	No	Comment
Choku-zuki	Shizentai	10	Facing forward
Gyaku-zuki	Zenkutsu	5	Left and right
Oi-zuki	Zenkutsu	5	Turn, same back
Age-uke	Zenkutsu	5	Turn, same back
Uchi-uke	Zenkutsu	5	Turn, same back
Gedan barai	Zenkutsu	5	Turn, same back
Mae-geri	Zenkutsu	5	Turn, same back

Kumite
Gohon kumite – 5 attack sparring (pages 206 and 207)
Upper level only to count

Kata
Taikyo-ku shodan
First half only, fast to count

N.B. Only English terminology will be used in this examination

9th KYU – RED BELT

Basics

Technique	Stance	No	Comment
Choku-zuki	Shizentai	10	Facing forward
Gyaku-zuki	Zenkutsu	5	Left and right
Oi-zuki	Zenkutsu	5	Turn, same back
Age-uke	Zenkutsu	5	Turn, same back
Soto-ude-uke	Zenkutsu	5	Turn, same back
Uchi-uke	Zenkutsu	5	Turn, same back
Mae-geri	Zenkutsu	5	Turn, same back
Yoko geri keage	Kiba	3	Turn, same back
Yoko geri kekomi	Kiba	3	Turn, same back

Kumite
Gohon kumite – Jōdan and Chūdan no count (pages 206–209)

Kata
Taikyo-ku Shodan
Fast no count

8th KYU – ORANGE BELT

Basics

Technique	Stance	No	Comment
Choku-zuki	Shizentai	10	Facing forward
Gyaku-zuki	Zenkutsu	5	Left and right
Oi-zuki	Zenkutsu	5	Forward and back
Age-uke	Zenkutsu	5	Forward and back
Soto-ude-uke	Zenkutsu	5	Forward and back
Uchi-uke	Zenkutsu	5	Forward and back
Shutō uke	Kōkutsu	5	Forward and back
Mae-geri	Zenkutsu	5	Turn, same back
Yoko geri keage	Kiba	3	Turn, same back
Yoko geri kekomi	Kiba	3	Turn, same back

Kumite
Kihon ippon kumite – Set 1 (page 270)
Attack Jōdan, Chūdan, Mae-geri from left stance followed by the
same from right stance (one attack at each level)

Kata
Heian shodan, plus any previous kata

7th KYU – YELLOW BELT

Basics

Technique	Stance	No	Comment
Oi-zuki	Zenkutsu	5	Forward and back
Age-uke/Gyaku-zuki	Zenkutsu	5	Forward and back
Soto-ude-uke/ Gyaku-zuki	Zenkutsu	5	Forward and back
Uchi-uke/Gyaku-zuki	Zenkutsu	5	Forward and back
Shutō uke/Nukite	Kōkutsu	5	Forward and back
Mae-geri	Zenkutsu	5	Turn, same back
Yoko geri keage	Kiba	3	Turn, same back
Yoko geri kekomi	Kiba	3	Turn, same back

Kumite
Sanbon kumite, Attack Jōdan, Chūdan, Mae-geri (pages 219–223)
First perform attacks from left stance – then from right

Kata
Heian Nidan, plus any previous kata

6th KYU – GREEN BELT

Basics

Technique	No	Comment
Sanbon-zuki	5	Turn, same back
Age-uke/Gyaku-zuki/Gedan barai	5	Forward and back
Uchi-uke/Gyaku-zuki/Gedan barai	5	Forward and back
Shutō-uke/Mae-kizami-geri/Nukite	5	Forward and back
Ren-geri-jōdan-chūdan	3	Turn, Chūdan-jōdan
Yoko-geri-keage	3	Turn, same back
Yoko-geri-kekomi	3	Turn, same back
Mawashi-geri	5	Turn, same back

Kumite
Kihon ippon kumite – Set 2 (page 270)
Attack left Jōdan, Chūdan and Mae-geri, then repeat on the right

Kata
Heian sandan, plus any previous kata

5th KYU – PURPLE BELT

Basics

Technique	No	Comment
Sanbon-zuki	5	Forward and back
Age-uke/Mae-geri/Gyaku-zuki	5	Forward and back
Soto-ude-uke/Yoko Empi/Uraken	5	Forward and back
Uchi-uke/Kizami-zuki/Gyaku-zuki	5	Forward and back
Shutō-uke/Mae-kizami-geri/Nukite	5	Forward and back
Mae-geri/Oi-zuki	3	Turn, Mae-geri/Gyaku-zuki
Mae-ren-geri Chūdan, Jōdan	3	Turn, same Jōdan-chūdan
Ren-geri Mae-geri/Mawashi-geri	3	Turn, Mawashi-geri/Mae-geri
Ren-geri Mae-geri/Kekomi	3	Turn, Kekomi/Mae-geri

Kumite
Kihon ippon kumite – Set 3 (page 272)
Attack 5 different attacks with the left – then repeat on the right

Kata
Heian Yondan, plus any previous kata

4th KYU – PURPLE BELT WITH 2 WHITE STRIPES

Basics

		No
1.	Sanbon-zuki 5 times – *Turn* – Mae-geri/Sanbon-zuki	5
2.	Age-uke/Mae-geri/Gyaku-zuki/Gedan-barai *Stepping back the same*	5
3.	Soto-ude-uke/Yoko-empi/Uraken/Gyaku-zuki/Gedan-barai *Stepping back the same*	5
4.	Uchi-uki (Kōkutsu dachi), Kizami-zuki/Gyaku-zuki/ Gedan-barai (Zenkutsu dachi) *Stepping back the same*	5
5.	Shūto-uke/Mae-kizami-geri/Nukite *Stepping back the same*	5
6.	Mae-geri/Mawashi-geri/Uraken/Gyaku-zuki/Gedan-barai *Turn – same back*	3
7.	Mae-geri/Kekomi/Shūto-uchi/Gyaku-zuki/Gedan-barai *Turn – same back*	3
8.	Yoko-geri-keage (Kiba dachi), Gyaku-zuki (Zenkutsu dachi), Gedan-barai (Kiba dachi) *Turn – same back*	3

Kumite
Kihon ippon kumite – Set 4 (page 272)
Attack 5 different attacks with the left, then repeat on the right

Kata
Heian Godan, plus any previous kata

3rd KYU – BROWN BELT

Basics

		No
1.	Sanbon-zuki 5 times – *Turn* – Mae-geri/Sanbon-zuki	5
2.	Age-uke/Mae-geri/Gyaku-zuki/Gedan-barai *Stepping back the same*	5
3.	Soto-ude-uke/Yoko-empi/Uraken/Gyaku-zuki/Gedan-barai *Stepping back the same*	5
4.	Uchi-uki (Kōkutsu dachi), Kizami-zuki/Gyaku-zuki/ Gedan barai (Zenkutsu dachi) *Stepping back the same*	5
5.	Shutō-uke/Mae-kizami-geri/Nukite *Stepping back the same*	5
6.	Mae-geri/Mawashi-geri/Uraken/Gyaku-zuki/Gedan-barai *Turn – same back*	3
7.	Mae-geri/Kekomi/Shutō-uchi/Gyaku-zuki/Gedan-barai *Turn – same back*	3
8.	Yoko-geri-keage (Kiba dachi), Gyaku-zuki (Zenkutsu dachi), Gedan-barai (Kiba dachi) *Turn – same back*	3
9.	Ushiro geri from Zenkutsu dachi *Turn – same back*	3
10.	Face the front in Zenkutsu dachi Mae-geri to the front, kekomi to the side with same leg *Same with opposite leg*	3

Kumite

Kihon ippon kumite – Set 5 (page 272)
Attack 5 times with the left side, then repeat on the right

Jiyu-ippon-kumite – Set 1 (page 273)
Attack with right side only – Jōdan, chūdan and mae-geri

Kata

Tekki Shodan, plus any previous kata

2nd KYU – BROWN BELT WITH 2 WHITE STRIPES

Basics

No

1. Sanbon-zuki 5 times – *Turn* – Mae-geri/Sanbon-zuki   5

2. Age-uke/Mae-geri/Gyaku-zuki/Gedan-barai   5
   Stepping back the same

3. Soto-ude-uke/Yoko-empi/Uraken/Gyaku-zuki/Gedan-barai   5
   Stepping back the same

4. Uchi-uki (Kōkutsu dachi), Kizami-zuki/Gyaku-zuki/   5
   Gedan-barai (Zenkutsu dachi)
   Stepping back the same

5. Shutō-uke/Mawashi-kizami-geri/Nukite   5
   Stepping back the same

6. Mae-geri/Mawashi-geri/Uraken/Gyaku-zuki/Gedan-barai   3
   Turn – same back

7. Mae-geri/Kekomi/Shutō-uchi/Gyaku-zuki/Gedan-barai   3
   Turn – same back

8. Yoko-geri-keage (Kiba dachi), Gyaku-zuki (Zenkutsu dachi),
   Gedan-barai (Kiba dachi)   3
   Turn – same back

9. Ushiro-geri/Gyaku-zuki   3
   Turn – same back

10. Face the front in Zenkutsu dachi. Mae-geri/Kekomi with
    the same leg. Mae-geri/Mawashi-geri with the same leg   3
    Same with opposite leg

Kumite
Kihon-ippon-kumite (page 272). Any set of the examiner's choice.
Attacking from both sides

Jiyu-ippon-kumite – Set 2 (page 273). Attack with both sides,
jōdan, chūdan and mae-geri

Kata
Bassai Dai, plus any previous kata

1st KYU – BROWN BELT WITH 2 RED STRIPES

Basics

		No
1.	Sanbon-zuki 5 times – *Turn* – Mae-geri/Sanbon-zuki	5
2.	Age-uke/Mae-geri/Gyaku-zuki/Gedan-barai *Stepping back the same*	5
3.	Soto-ude-uke/Yoko-empi/Uraken/Gyaku-zuki/Gedan-barai *Stepping back the same*	5
4.	Uchi-uki (Kōkutsu dachi), Kizami-zuki/Gyaku-zuki/ Gedan-barai (Zenkutsu dachi) *Stepping back the same*	5
5.	Shutō-uke/Mawashi-kizami-geri/Nukite *Stepping back the same*	5
6.	Mae-geri/Mawashi-geri/Uraken/Gyaku-zuki/Gedan-barai *Turn – same back*	3
7.	Mae-geri/Kekomi/Shutō-uchi/Gyaku-zuki/Gedan-barai *Turn – same back*	3
8.	Yoko-geri-keage (Kiba dachi), Gyaku-zuki (Zenkutsu dachi), Gedan-barai (Kiba dachi) *Turn – same back*	3
9.	Ushiro-geri/Gyaku-zuki *Turn – same back*	3
10.	Kekomi (front leg), Mae-geri (back leg), step forward *Turn – same back*	3
11.	Face the front in Zenkutsu dachi. Mae-geri/Kekomi with the same leg. Mae-geri/Mawashi-geri with the same leg. Mae-geri/Kekomi/Ushiro-geri with the same leg *Same with opposite leg*	3

Kumite

Kihon-ippon-kumite – Sets 1–5 (page 272). Right attack only

Jiyu-ippon-kumite – Set 3 (page 273). Left attacks first,
followed by right attacks

Kata

A choice of one of the following:
Kanku-dai, Enpi, Jion, Jitte, Ji'in, plus any previous kata

SHODAN – BLACK BELT. 1st DEGREE

All Kihon and combination techniques are performed from Jiyu dachi

Basics   **No**

1. Kizami-zuki/Mae-geri/Sanbon-zuki. *Turn same back*   3

2. Age-uke/Mae-geri/Gyaku-zuki/Gedan-barai   5
   Stepping back the same

3. Soto-ude-uke/Yoko-empi/Uraken/Gyaku-zuki/Gedan-barai   5
   Stepping back the same

4. Uchi-uke (Kōkutsu dachi), Kizami-zuki/Gyaku-zuki/   5
   Gedan-barai
   Stepping back the same

5. Shūto-uke/Mawashi-kizami-geri/Nukite   5
   Stepping back the same

6. Mae-geri/Mawashi-geri/Uraken/Gyaku-zuki/Gedan-barai   3
   Turn – same back

7. Mae-geri/Kekomi/Shutō-uchi/Gyaku-zuki/Gedan-barai   3
   Turn – same back

8. Gyaku-zuki/Mae-geri/Mawashi-geri/Turn/Shutō-uke/Gyaku-zuki 3
   Turn – same back

9. Step back, Age-uke, step forward Mawashi-geri (back leg), 3
   Uraken/Oi-zuki. *Turn same back*

10. Mawashi-kizami-geri/Ushiro-geri/Uraken/Gyaku-zuki   3
    Turn – same back

11. Kizami kekomi, step forward Mae-geri/Oi-zuki/Gyaku-zuki 3
    Turn – same back

12. Stepping in Kiba dachi, Keage/Kekomi with the same leg   3
    Turn – same back

13. Face the front in Zenkusu dachi. Mae-geri/Kekomi/Ushiro-geri 3
    Repeat on opposite side

Kumite
Kihon-ippon-kumite – Sets 1–5, attacking from both sides.
Jiyu-ippon-kumite – Sets 1–5, attacking from both sides.
Freestyle sparring (Jiyu kumite) against two consecutive dan grades.

Kata
A choice of one of the following:
Kanku-dai, Enpi, Jion, Jitte, Ji'in, Gankaku or Hangetsu
plus previous kata
Oral examination to assess student's character.

NIDAN – BLACK BELT. 2nd DEGREE

Basics

Basics are the same as for Shodan with the addition of:

Kizami kekomi/Ushiro geri/Shutō uchi/Gyaku zuki three times. Turn same back.

On the same leg, Mae geri/Kekomi/Ushiro geri/Mawashi geri and return to the starting position. Repeat on the other side.

Kumite

Jiyu ippon kumite. Sets 1–5, attack from both sides.

Okuri jiyu ippon kumite (two attacks), first specified, second free.

Specified attacks are: one Jōdan, one Chūdan, one Mae geri, one Kekomi, one Mawashi geri and one Ushiro geri.

Jiyu kumite against three consecutive dan grades of Nidan status.

Kata

Tokui kata with explanation of Bunkai.

Plus any previous kata.

Oral examination as in Shodan.

SANDAN – BLACK BELT. 3rd DEGREE

Basics

Demonstration of all basic Shotokan techniques against a stationary target.

Kumite

Jiyu kumite against five consecutive Sandans. Minimum non-stop fighting time: 10 minutes.

Kata

Tokui kata plus interpretation of Bunkai.

Any other previous kata of the examiner's choice.

Demonstration of teaching ability.

Oral examination as in Nidan.

KIHON IPPON KUMITE – COMPULSORY DEFENCES
All defences listed below are against a right hand or foot attack

SET 1
Attacks: Jōdan/Chūdan/Mae-geri (one of each, right and left)

Defences:
Jōdan No. 1   Hidari-jōdan age-uke/Migi-chūdan, gyaku-zuki
Chūdan No. 1   Hidari-chūdan soto-ude-uke/Migi-chūdan, gyaku-zuki
Mae-geri No. 1   Hidari-gedan-barai/Migi-chūdan Gyaku-zuki

SET 2
Attacks: Jōdan/Chūdan/Mae-geri (one of each, right and left)

Defences:
Jōdan No.2   Hidari-jōdan-tate shutō-uke/Migi-jōdan, shutō-uchi
Chūdan No. 2   Migi-chūdan, soto-ude-uke/Migi-chūdan, yoko-enpi-uchi
Mae-geri No. 2   Migi-gyaku gedan-barai/Hidari-jōdan, kizami-zuki/
     Migi-chūdan gyaku-zuki

SET 3
Attacks: Jōdan/Chūdan/Mae-geri/Kekomi/Mawashi-geri
     (one of each, right and left)

Defences:
Jōdan No. 3   Migi-jōdan age-uke/Migi-yoko-geri keage/Migi-chūdan
     yoko-enpi-uchi
Chūdan No. 3   Hidari-chūdan uchi-ude-uke/Hidari-jōdan, kizami-zuki/
     Migi-chūdan gyaku-zuki
Mae-geri No. 3   Migi-gedan juji-uke/Jōdan-shutō, juji-uchi
Kekomi No. 1   Hidari-chūdan soto-ude-uke/Migi-chūdan, gyaku-zuki
Mawashi-geri No. 1   Hidari-haiwan uchi-uke/Migi-chūdan, gyaku-zuki

SET 4
Attacks: Same as Set 3

Defences:
Jōdan No. 4   Hidari-jōdan haishu, juji-uke/Chūdan mawashi-geri/
     Hidari-jōdan ushiro, mawashi, enpi
Chūdan No. 4   Hidari-chūdan shutō-uke/Kizami, mae-geri/Migi-
     chūdan-tate yonhon-nukite
Mae-geri No. 4   Migi-gedan-barai/Hidari-gyaku-tate, shutō-uke/Migi-
     chūdan, mae-enpi
Kekomi No. 2   Hidari-chūdan kake-uke/Migi-jōdan haito-uchi
Mawashi-geri No. 2   Tate-heiko shutō-uke/Soete-yoko, enpi-uchi

SET 5
Attacks: Same as Set 3

Defences:
Jōdan No. 5   Hidari-jōdan age-uke/Migi-jōdan, mae-geri/Migi-jōdan,
     enpi-uchi
Chūdan No. 5   Hidari-chūdan enpi-uke/Migi-jōdan, ushiro, mawashi,
     enpi-uchi
Mae-geri No. 5   Hidari-chūdan sukui-uke/Migi-chūdan, gyaku-zuki
Kekomi No. 3   Migi-ushiro gedan-barai/Migi-chudan yoko-geri,
     Kekomi/Migi-yoko, enpi
Mawashi-geri No. 3   Migi-jōdan, soto-ude-uke/Mae-kizami-geri, Hidari-
     gyaku-zuki

JIYU IPPON KUMITE – COMPULSORY DEFENCES

All defences listed below are against a right hand or foot attack

SET 1

Attacks: Jōdan/Chūdan/Mae-geri (one of each, right only)

Defences:

Jōdan No. 1 — Hidari-jōdan-tate shutō-uke/Migi-chūdan gyaku-zuki/ Hikite-gamae

Chūdan No. 1 — Hidari-chūdan soto-ude-uke/Migi-chūdan, gyaku-zuki/ Hikite-gamae

Mae-geri No. 1 — Hidari-gedan-barai/Migi-chūdan gyaku-zuki/Hikite-gamae

SET 2

Attacks: Jōdan/Chūdan/Mae-geri (one of each, right and left)

Defences:

Jōdan No.2 — Hidari-jōdan nagashi-uke/Migi-chūdan ura-zuki/ Hikite-gamae

Chūdan No. 2 — Hidari-seiryuto gedan-uke/Migi-jōdan uraken-uchi/ Hikite-gamae

Mae-geri No. 2 — Migi-gedan-barai/Hidari-gyaku, tate-shutō/Migi-jōdan choku-zuki/Hikite-gamae

SET 3

Attacks: Jōdan/Chūdan/Mae-geri/Kekomi/Mawashi-geri (one of each, right and left)

Defences:

Jōdan No. 3 — Migi-jōdan, age-uke/Migi-kizami, mawashi-geri/Hidari-chūdan gyaku-zuki/Hikite-gamae

Chūdan No. 3 — Hidari-gyaku-zuki/Hikite-gamae

Mae-geri No. 3 — Hidari-gedan juji-uke/Hidari-yoko, shutō-uchi/Hikite-gamae

Kekomi No. 1 — Hidari soto-ude-uke/Migi-chudan gyaku-zuki/Hikite-gamae

Mawashi-geri No. 1 — Hidari-jōdan haiwan-uke/Migi-chūdan, gyaku-zuki/ Hikite-gamae

SET 4

Attacks: Same as Set 3

Defences:

Jōdan No. 4 — Hidari-hirate-barai/Migi-teisho-uchi/Hikite-barai

Chūdan No. 4 — Migi-chūdan mae-geri/Hidari-gedan-barai/Kamae/ Hidari-jōdan kizami-zuki, Zanshin-gamae

Mae-geri No. 4 — Migi-gedan-osae nagashi-uke/Hidari-chūdan gyaku-zuki/Hikite-gamae

Kekomi No. 2 — Awase-seiryuto-uke/Migi-jōdan tate-zuki/Zanshin-gamae

Mawashi-geri No. 2 — Hidari-jōdan-kizami gyaku-zuki/Migi-tate shutō-uke

SET 5

Attacks: Same as Set 3

Defences:

Jōdan No. 5 — Hidari-osae-uke/Migi-tobi-geri/Uraken-uchi

Chūdan No. 5 — Migi-gyaku gedan-barai/Migi-jōdan-ushiro mawashi-geri/Migi-ashi-barai/Migi-gyaku-zuki/Hikite-gamae

Mae-geri No. 5 — Migi-gedan-barai/Hidari-gyaku tate-shutō/Hidari-ashi-barai/Migi-gyaku-zuki/Hikite-gamae

Kekomi No. 3 — Hidari-kake-uke (Haiwan)/Ushiro-mawashi, enpi/Zanshin-gamae

Mawashi-geri No. 3 — Awase-shuto-uke and Migi-jodan-kizami mawashi-geri

PART 4
SELF DEFENCE
WOMEN IN KARATE

Just as we have seen a huge increase in the number of children taking up Karate, so too has the number of women being attracted to the art increased. Twenty-five years ago, women made up about **2%** of the total class, whereas today, that figure is nearer **20%**. The reasons for this are not difficult to understand.

Year by year there has been a disturbing increase in crimes of violence. Rape has become widespread, so much so that "rape within the confines of marriage" has become an indictable offence, where once it never could, due to changes in the law to protect the female. Muggings and sexual attacks have become commonplace, and as the law does not allow a person to carry a weapon, is it any wonder women are turning to karate in their thousands?

Karate training will **not** make a woman muscle-bound, for being Arnold Schwarzenegger's female counterpart is not most women's idea of a body beautiful (nor is it most men's, come to that). On the contrary, it will tone the muscles, firm the body and generally make her more feminine and appealing.

Add to that a pastime that is inexpensive – one that can be practised alone and gives a marvellous outlet for frustration and aggression – together with the chance to meet some very nice like-minded people, then the argument **for** women in karate is overwhelming.

ATTACKER GRABS BOTH WRISTS.

IF HE IS STRONG, FIRST KICK TO THE GROIN.

STEP FORWARD AND WITH BOTH HANDS PUSH ATTACKER AWAY.

ALTERNATIVE COUNTER ATTACK NO.1 GRAB THE ATTACKER'S RIGHT WRIST WITH THE LEFT HAND.

STEP IN STRIKING THE NECK WITH A KNIFE HAND STRIKE.

OPPONENT GRABS THE RIGHT WRIST.

TWIST PALMS UPWARDS TO BREAK GRIP.

AS GRIP IS RELEASED PREPARE TO PUSH.

STEP IN AND ATTACK TO THE CHIN WITH A PALM HEEL STRIKE. DO NOT LET GO OF THE RIGHT WRIST.

ALTERNATIVE COUNTER ATTACK NO.2 HOLDING THE WRIST, BRING THE RIGHT HAND TO THE LEFT EAR.

MAKE A FIST WITH THE RIGHT HAND AND TAKE HOLD OF IT WITH THE LEFT. START THE ATTACK BY TWISTING...

THE ATTACKER'S ARM IN ON HIMSELF AND FINISH WITH A RISING ELBOW STRIKE TO THE CHIN.

5

ATTACKER GRABS RIGHT WRIST.

PULL BACK AND BREAK THE GRIP.

ALTERNATIVE STRIKE NO.1 IS A BACKFIST
TO THE RIBCAGE. HERE THE ARM SWINGS
LATERALLY.

6

ALTERNATIVE STRIKE NO.2 IS AN UPWARD
BACKFIST STRIKE TO THE GROIN.

8

ATTACKER COMES FROM BEHIND

WITH A BEAR HUG OVER THE CHEST.

CONTINUE MOVING THE RIGHT ARM IN A CIRCULAR MOTION.

STEP IN AND STRIKE TO THE BRIDGE OF THE NOSE WITH A BACKFIST STRIKE.

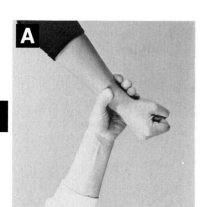

CLOSE-UP VIEW SHOWING THE GRAB...

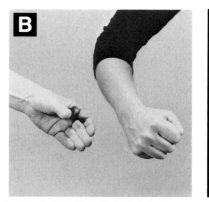

AND THE BREAK BETWEEN THE THUMB AND FINGERS.

DROP THE BODY LOW, SIMULTANEOUSLY RAISING BOTH ELBOWS TO BREAK THE GRIP.

COUNTER ATTACK TO THE SOLAR PLEXUS WITH A REVERSE ELBOW STRIKE, AUGMENTED WITH THE LEFT HAND.

279

9

ATTACKER PREPARES TO ATTACK FROM BEHIND.

USING A BEAR HUG LOW DOWN, HE TRAPS THE UPPER ARMS.

10

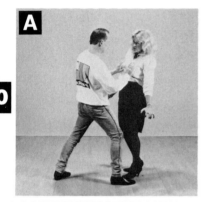

IN A QUITE UNFORGIVABLE ACTION, THE ATTACKER MAKES HIS MOVE.

MAINTAINING HER DISTANCE, SHE SWINGS BOTH ARMS BACKWARDS...

11

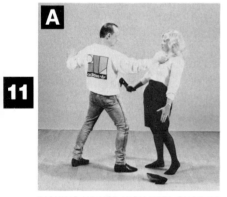

PICKING UP HER HIGH HEEL SHOE TO PROTECT HERSELF FROM THIS MUCH STRONGER MAN...

SHE STRIKES WITH HER FINGERS TO THE EYES.

STILL ABLE TO MOVE HER LOWER RIGHT ARM SHE TWISTS HER BODY TO THE LEFT,

STRIKING THE UNPROTECTED GROIN WITH A KNIFEHAND STRIKE.

AND THEN FORWARDS, STRIKING BOTH ARMS SIMULTANEOUSLY ABOVE THE ELBOW JOINTS.

BOTH ARMS ARE BROKEN BY THE FORCE OF THE PALM HEEL STRIKES.

USING THE HEEL AS A WEAPON

SHE DRIVES IT INTO THE MAN'S EYE: NORMALLY, NO ONE WOULD DREAM OF EVER DOING THIS. BUT IN A LIFE AND DEATH SITUATION, MANY WOULD.

281

HERE BASIC BLOCKS ARE USED TO GREAT ADVANTAGE. SOTO UDE UKE, AGE UKE, GEDAN BARAI AND KAKEWAKI UKE.

12

THE VICTIM IS GRABBED BY THE LEFT LAPEL.

USING THE TWISTING ACTION OF THE HIPS STEPPING BACK – SHE ATTACKS ABOVE THE ELBOW JOINT WITH SOTO UDE UKE.

15

THE ATTACKER GRABS THE RIGHT LAPEL.

STEPPING IN...

16

FROM THE FRONT, BOTH LAPELS ARE HELD.

USING A WEDGE BLOCK, PRISE BOTH ARMS APART. IF THE ATTACKER IS TOO STRONG FRONT GROIN KICK WOULD NOT GO AMISS

282

THE ABOVE PHOTOGRAPH SHOWS THE SAME
ATTACK BEING THWARTED BY AN AGE UKE.

THE MOMENT AN UPPER RISING BLOCK ON
THE OTHER SIDE BECOMES AN ATTACK.

A RIGHT DOWNWARD BLOCK IS DELIVERED
TO THE CROOK OF THE ARM, CAUSING THE
ATTACKER TO INCLINE FORWARD.

THIS BRINGS HIS NECK INTO THE PERFECT
POSITION FOR A DOWNWARD ELBOW
STRIKE. (OTOSHI EMPI)

STEPPING THROUGH...

SWING THE RIGHT ARM IN A BIG ARC AND
STRIKE THE GROIN WITH A RIDGE HAND
STRIKE. (HAITO UCHI)

283

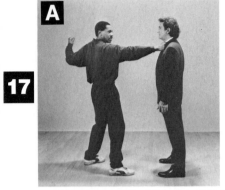

THE AGGRESSOR TAKES HOLD OF THE LEFT LAPEL.

TAKE HOLD OF HIS RIGHT THUMB AND ATTACK TO THE EYES.

KEEP HOLD OF THE RIGHT HAND AS A WRIST LOCK CAN BE APPLIED. KICK WITH THE RIGHT LEG TO THE RIBS.

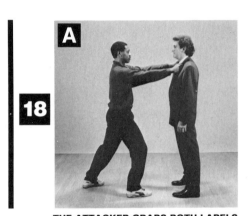

THE ATTACKER GRABS BOTH LAPELS.

DISTRACT HIM BY FIRST ATTACKING TO THE EYES WITH THE RIGHT AND THEN LEFT.

SWEEP HIS RIGHT ARM ACROSS AND DOWN APPLYING AN ARM LOCK.

284

BRING THE RIGHT HAND UP FOR ADDITIONAL
SUPPORT AND TWIST OUTWARDS.

SIMULTANEOUSLY STEP BEHIND WITH THE
LEFT FOOT, USE THE HIPS AND THROW.

IF HE IS VERY STRONG MAKE A SLIGHT
ADJUSTMENT TO THE POSITION OF HIS
TESTICLES

SWING BOTH ARMS UP AS IF PERFORMING
TWO AGE UKES TOGETHER.

WITH THE LEFT HAND GRAB HIS HAIR

AND PULL HIS HEAD RIGHT BACK,
SiMULTANEOUSLY BRINGING THE LEFT KNEE
UP TO ATTACK HIS NECK.

285

IF THE HAIR IS PULLED FROM THE FRONT

BRING BOTH HANDS ON TOP OF THE ATTACKER'S HAND AND PULL DOWN TO RELIEVE THE PAIN.

BRING THE RIGHT HAND OVER AND TAKE HOLD OF THE LITTLE FINGER SIDE OF HIS HAND.

BRING THE LEFT HAND ON TO THE ATTACKER'S ARM FOR SUPPORT AND, AS THAT PROMINENT INSTRUCTOR MICK NURSEY WAS HEARD TO SAY,"LOOSEN HIM UP".

IF THE RIGHT WRIST SHOULD BE GRABBED

EXPAND THE FINGERS OF THE RIGHT HAND. THIS INCREASES THE WRIST GIRTH, SO LESSENING THE ATTACKER'S GRIP.

USING THE BACK LEG, SWING IT FORWARD AND UP INTO HIS GROIN.

20

IF THE LEFT LAPEL SHOULD BE GRIPPED

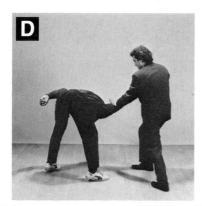

WITH BOTH HANDS, SWING THE RIGHT ARM INTO AN ARMLOCK (BY SLIDING THE LEFT HAND ABOVE THE ELBOW JOINT).

FINALLY, KICK TO THE FACE WITH THE RIGHT INSTEP.

TWIST THE OPEN RIGHT HAND UPWARDS, SO PUTTING PRESSURE ON HIS WRIST.

MOVE IN AND APPLY AN AUGMENTED UPPER RISING ELBOW STRIKE TO THE CHIN.

A

22

THE ASSAILANT GRABS THE HAIR.

B

BRING THE LEFT HAND ON TOP OF HIS GRABBING HAND TO RELIEVE THE PRESSURE. BEGIN TO STEP IN.

E

BY PULLING SHARPLY TOWARDS YOU, THE ATTACKER WILL BE THROWN BACKWARDS AND BECOME AIRBORNE. (THIS IS NOT THE TIME TO ENQUIRE WHETHER OR NOT HE HAS A PILOT'S LICENCE).

F

INSTEAD...

A

23

THE ATTACKER LAUNCHES A RUGBY-STYLE TACKLE AT YOUR WAIST.

B

SLIDE THE RIGHT ARM UNDER HIS LEFT AND THE LEFT HAND BEHIND HIS HEAD.

288

STEP IN AND DROP DOWN, PUNCHING TO THE GROIN.

BEFORE HE CAN RECOVER, QUICKLY CLASP BOTH HANDS BEHIND HIS KNEES.

FOLLOW SUIT YOURSELF BY LEAPING INTO THE AIR AND...

LANDING ON HIS CHEST, BRING YOUR THUMBS INTO HIS EYES.

STEPPING BACK – CONTINUE HIS FORWARD MOMENTUM BY TWISTING AND THROWING.

STRIKE WITH A KNIFE HAND STRIKE TO THE THROAT OR NECK.

A

THE ATTACKER GRABS THE LEFT SHOULDER
FROM THE SIDE.

B

CATCH UNDER HIS RIGHT ARM AND
COUNTER ATTACK TO THE EYES.

E

CONTINUE SWEEPING AND PULLING.

F

AUTOMATICALLY, THE RIGHT HAND WILL
COME ON TOP READY FOR THE FINISHING
MOVE.

B

STEP THROUGH AND TO HIS RIGHT, TWIST
THE ARM (BACK OF FIST DOWN), EXECUTING
AN ARM LEVER USING YOUR SHOULDER AS
A FULCRUM.

C

AFTER BREAKING THE ARM – STRIKE WITH A
LEFT REVERSE ROUNDHOUSE ELBOW STRIKE

290

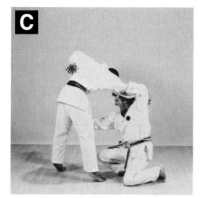

C

DROP DOWN ON TO ONE KNEE AND PUNCH
TO THE GROIN.

D

BRING THE RIGHT ARM DOWN IN A
SCOOPING ACTION, AS CONTACT WITH THE
LEG IS MADE, PULL DOWN WITH THE LEFT
HAND.

G

STRIKE IMMEDIATELY WITH A KNIFE HAND
STRIKE TO THE NECK OR THROAT.

25

A

BLOCK AN UPPER PUNCH WITH AN X BLOCK
AS THE RIGHT LEG MOVES BACK.

D

PIVOT ON THE LEFT FOOT AND SWEEP HIS
FRONT LEG WITH YOUR RIGHT LEG.

E

QUICKLY COUNTER ATTACK USING THE
FOOT EDGE TO THE RIB CAGE.

**BLOCK AN UPPER PUNCH USING AN
X BLOCK.**

**TWIST THE ARM TO THE RIGHT AND DOWN
IN A CIRCULAR MOTION.**

**KEEP HOLD WITH YOUR LEFT HAND AND
SWING YOUR RIGHT ARM OVER HIS CHEST
AND BEHIND HIS HEAD.**

**AT THIS POINT HE IS COMPLETELY
POWERLESS. QUICKLY WITHDRAW THE LEFT
HAND AND...**

TURN IN AND STRIKE TO THE EYES.

**RELEASE HIS GRIP BY EXECUTING A LEFT
UPPER RISING BLOCK.**

STEP THROUGH TO THE OUTSIDE UNDER THE ARM YOU ARE HOLDING. TURN TO YOUR LEFT AND BRING HIS ARM UP HIS BACK.

AS HE TRIES TO ATTACK WITH HIS ONLY FREE ARM DUCK UNDER HIS BACK FIST STRIKE...

STRIKE WITH A BOTTOM FIST STRIKE TO THE GROIN.

27

BEING GRABBED FROM THE SIDE.

CATCH HIS RIGHT ARM WITH YOUR LEFT AND BRING YOUR RIGHT HAND BEHIND HIS NECK.

PULL HIS HEAD FORWARD, BRINGING HIS FACE IN CONTACT WITH YOUR RIGHT KNEE.

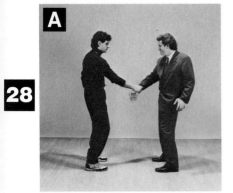

A

28

IN GOOD FAITH, YOU OFFER YOUR HAND TO
SHAKE HANDS. INSTEAD – YOUR WRIST IS
GRABBED.

B

PLACE YOUR LEFT HAND ON THE BACK OF
HIS.

A

29

IN THE BEAR HUG FROM BEHIND, THE ARMS
REMAIN FREE.

B

PRISE YOUR RIGHT HAND UNDER HIS LITTLE
FINGER.

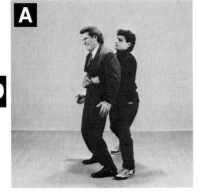

A

30

A BEAR HUG THAT LEAVES THE ARMS
UNENCUMBERED.

B

LOOK AT THE BACK OF THE UPPERMOST
HAND AND RAISE THE RIGHT FIST.

TWIST YOUR RIGHT HAND IN A CLOCKWISE CIRCULAR MOTION KEEPING THE LEFT HAND IN PLACE.

TAKE HOLD OF HIS RIGHT WRIST AND ROLL IT TOWARDS HIM. THIS ROLLING ACTION HAS AN AMAZING EFFECT ON THE KNEES AND CAUSES THEM TO BUCKLE.

HOLDING IT TIGHTLY, RIP IT BACKWARDS ACROSS YOUR BODY.

CLOSE-UP SHOT OF THE LITTLE FINGER JUST PRIOR TO DISLOCATION.

STRIKE INTO THE CENTRE OF THE BACK OF THE HAND WITH A ONE-KNUCKLE FIST. REPEAT IF NECESSARY.

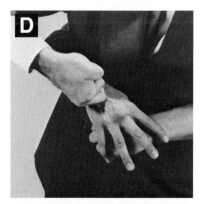

CLOSE-UP OF A ONE-KNUCKLE FIST "MASSAGING" A VITAL SPOT.

Have you ever shaken hands with, (fortunately they are in a minority group) men who proceed to crush your hand in an effort to convince you they are very strong. What is more galling, is that their bone crushing antics are usually accompanied by a beaming smile. Uncannily, that smile remains intact for the whole duration of the greeting, causing our complex ridden chum to take on the guise of an amateur ventriloquist. The following defences will "Wipe the smile off his face".

THE JAPANESE "BOW" WESTERNERS "SHAKE HANDS"

TWIST HIS HAND TURNING THE RIGHT PALM UPWARDS. STEP IN BRINGING THE LEFT ARM OVER HIS RIGHT.

YOUR LEFT ARM IS NOW BEAUTIFULLY POSITIONED FOR AN ELBOW STRIKE.
(BUT REMEMBER, YOU MAY WISH TO DO BUSINESS WITH THIS CHAP AND CONDUCTING IT FROM A HOSPITAL BED, MAY NOT ENHANCE YOUR CHANCES OF SUCCESS).

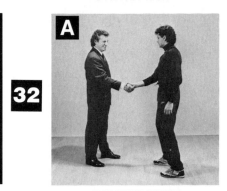

THE HANDSHAKE.

KEEPING HOLD OF HIS RIGHT HAND SWING YOUR RIGHT LEG UP READY FOR A HEEL KICK.

STRIKE HIS RIB CAGE WITH THE HEEL OF YOUR SHOE.

iously, meeting someone for the first time, despite their little problem does not give you the right to change his ysical appearance. The following defences taken "Just so far" will serve to remind him you have more up your eve than your arm.

ARRY ON DOWN IN A CIRCULAR ACTION.

SUPPORT HIS ARM UNDERNEATH BUT ABOVE THE ELBOW JOINT. PUSH DOWN WITH YOUR RIGHT HAND TO BREAK HIS ARM.

EAVE YOUR HAND IN HIS AND BEGIN TO JRN TO YOUR LEFT A COMPLETE CIRCLE, NGING YOUR LEFT HAND ON TO HIS RIGHT.

WITH HIS LOSS OF BALANCE TWIST BOTH HANDS OUTWARDS.

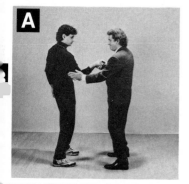

ACE THE LEFT HAND ON THE OUTSIDE OF HIS RIGHT ELBOW.

PUSH IN WITH THE LEFT HAND WHILE TWISTING OUT AND APPLYING A WRIST LOCK WITH THE RIGHT.

297

A

34

"THE PENNY HAS DROPPED" THIS IS NO
ORDINARY HAND-SHAKE SO FIRSTLY RAISE
THE LEFT HAND TO THE RIGHT EAR.

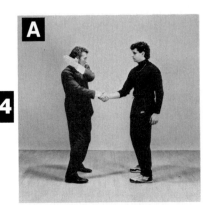

B

A SUCCESSFUL DISENGAGEMENT HERE
DEPENDS ON TIMING. THE KNIFE HAND STR
TO THE CROOK OF THE ARM MUST COINCID
WITH THE WITHDRAWAL OF THE RIGHT HAN

A

35

THE OPPONENT GRABS YOUR RIGHT WRIST
WITH TWO HANDS.

B

MOVE IN A LITTLE, MAKE A FIST WITH YO
RIGHT HAND, PASS YOUR LEFT ARM
BETWEEN HIS ARMS AND HOLD YOUR FIS

A

36

THE ATTACKER GRABS THE RIGHT WRIST

B

USE THE STRONG MUSCLES ON THE RIG
HAND SIDE OF THE BODY TO HELP
WITHDRAW THE HAND TO THE WAIST.

POWER SHOULD BE DIVIDED EQUALLY. 50% TO THE STRIKING HAND AND 50% TO THE WITHDRAWING ONE.

YOU ARE NOW IN A PERFECT POSITION TO DELIVER A STRAIGHT PUNCH – SHOULD IT BE NECESSARY.

TURN HIS HANDS BACK ON HIMSELF BY MOVING THE RIGHT ARM UP.

STEP RIGHT IN AND COMPLETE AN AUGMENTED UPPER RISING ELBOW STRIKE TO THE CHIN.

LOCK THE RIGHT HAND AT THE WAIST AND PIVOTING, TWIST THE HIPS SO THE STANCE FACES OUTWARDS. THE HAND IS EASILY RELEASED.

TWIST THE HIPS BACK BUT THIS TIME LET A BACK FIST STRIKE ACCOMPANY THEM.

ATTACKER COMES FROM THE REAR

AND PERFORMS A BEAR HUG VERY LOW DOWN TRAPPING HER ARMS COMPLETELY

SNAPPING HER LOWER RIGHT LEG UPWARDS, HER STILLETTO HEEL SCORES A DIRECT HIT ON ONE OF TWO TARGETS.

THIS IS THE PHOTOGRAPH THAT, WHEN TAKEN, BROUGHT TEARS TO THE CAMERAMAN'S EYES.

THE DOJO KUN
MORALS OF THE DOJO

"Dojo Kun"

"Hitotsu! Jinkaku Kansei ni Tsutomuru Koto"
(One! To Strive For The Perfection of Character!)

"Hitotsu! Makoto No Michi O Mamoru Koto!"
(One! To Defend The Paths Of Truth!)

"Hitotsu! Doryoku No Seishin O Yashinau Koto!"
(One! To Foster The Spirit Of Effort!)

"Hitotsu! Reigi O Omonzuru Koto!"
(One! To Honour The Principles of Etiquette!)

"Hitotsu! Kekki No Yu O Imashimuru Koto!"
(One! To Guard Against Impetuous Courage!)

The "Dojo Kun" is the Oath of the Karateka. Even today, it is recited at the end of each lesson at the Tokyo Headquarters of the Japan Karate Association, along with other Dojos in the J.K.A. Outside Japan I have not heard it, other than at training sessions of the Traditional Association of Shotokan Karate in Great Britain.

At the end of each lesson, the students and instructors line up to take the formal bow or "Rei", but before this and the usual "Mokuso" period, the whole class will sit in "Seiza" facing a shrine dedicated to Funakoshi Sensei.

The Dojo Captain or Senior Grade at the end of the two lines will shout out the "Dojo Kun", line at a time and immediately, the whole class will repeat each line back.

The Oath should always be chanted with strength, never mumbled in insincerity, for just as Karate movements should become automatic and reflexes conditioned, the simple Truths of the Oath should also penetrate the mind of the participant.

The "Dojo Kun" embodies all we are trying to achieve through the physical efforts of Karate training.

HOW TO CHOOSE A CLUB

Finding the right club for you can be a very hit or miss affair. It is possible to "make a go of it" with almost any club, instructor or style, but a little homework initially reduces the chances of you "dropping out" in the early stages by joining a club with maximum appeal and suitable to your personality and character. I suggest you follow a simple process of elimination.

1. Decide geographically where you would like to train and how far you are prepared to travel.
2. Contact the Martial Arts Commission in London telephone 081-691 3433 and ask them for the names and addresses of reputable instructors and clubs in your chosen area.
3. Compile a list of local clubs by visiting sports centres and collecting newspaper advertisements.
4. Talk to friends or personal contacts who already belong to a club. They naturally will have a strong bias in favour of their own club, so take this on board. Now, armed with a list of recommended clubs and their training times, visit them personally.

If your preference is for **sport karate,** look at the instructor, his experience as a competitor, ability to teach and communicate his competition skills, the success of the club in tournaments both locally and nationally. Finally, if many of the students are "bandaged to the hilt", it's a pretty good indication that injuries occur quite regularly and before long you would become just another statistic. Having said that, if you still find yourself driven by some masochistic urge to join, firstly check to see that your life assurance premiums are paid up to date!

On the other hand, your preference may be for **traditional karate.** If so, the teacher should set a good example to his students through discipline, etiquette, control and humility. He should have the ability to communicate to the class and consider the needs and requirements of the student on an individual basis. The underlying philosophy of karate-dō should run through the lesson and the analogy made between modern day living and ancient thinking. Whatever type of karate you wish to follow, that old adage, "you can fool some of the people some of the time . . . . . . " would seem to apply. Generally, if a teacher is good, he will attract a lot of good people – so a fair indicator is the size of a club and the numbers training.

Time spent looking at various clubs and talking to people is never wasted and before you realise it, the pieces of the jigsaw will have slotted into place and your club will be chosen for you.

BASIC RULES OF ETIQUETTE

Theoretically, the etiquette of karate-dō should not differ regardless of style, dojō, association or country – *but of course it does.* Bearing that in mind, a few simple rules will stand the beginner in good stead and should not cause any offence to his own instructor, and that is *very important.*

As basically a military art, karate puts great store in its ranking system. All belts are *earned*, not given away or bought, so the appropriate respect should be shown at all times.

1. Always be **punctual.**
2. Make sure your practice suit (Gi) is **clean** and folded correctly.
3. Smoking, eating or drinking is **not** permitted in the dojo.
4. **Toe** and **finger** nails should be cut regularly so as to prevent injury to other members.
5. **All** jewellery and personal adornments should be removed prior to training.
6. Do not **arrive** at the dojo in your "Karate Gi". Change into it when you get there.
7. Always bow to instructors and fellow students when seeing them for the **first time** and when departing.
8. Always remember the onus is on the **lower grade** to bow first.
9. Bow upon **entering** and **leaving** the dojo.
10. Bow before **joining** or **leaving** a class.
11. Bow after an instructor has **explained** something or **corrected** you.
12. In Japan, a student will enter a dojo and bow to all the instructors individually in order of **grade seniority**.
13. Always be polite and courteous to other karate-ka and extend this to **outside** the dojo.
14. On meeting a fellow karate-ka outside the dojo, a small low key but **correct bow** would not be out of place.
15. Endeavour to learn the "dojo kun" and incorporate it into your **daily life.**

The word "Oss" often accompanies a bow but in general, is only said to **people**. It is not usually said to inanimate objects.

One could quite easily fill a whole book when dealing with such a complex subject as Japanese protocol and etiquette. No one should reprimand you *severely* if your attitude is correct but you make a mistake out of ignorance. The Japanese are extremely polite people, but then again, they have had a lot of practice.

Just remember, **"manners are consideration for others"**, *and you will not go far wrong.*

PREPARING FOR GRADING

"The first grading will be the worst, after that, you'll have nothing to worry about". That remark was made by a well-known instructor. I must confess, I never did agree with him, and nor would anyone with an iota of common sense.

Grading examinations are, in the main, **very traumatic occasions.** Children, on the whole, cope quite well, being used to frequent exams at school, whereas with many adults, it may be literally years since they sat any kind of examination. Older students tend to worry the most. On balance they take things more seriously, for they want to do a good job having **less time left** in which to do it. On grading day, a small percentage of people wonder what on earth they are doing there and begin to question their own sanity. Of course, to be blasé or over-confident prior to an exam, would be a mistake. You need to be keyed up and just a little anxious for the adrenalin to flow and so give your best.

Most karate associations nowadays conduct gradings four times a year, enabling students to exchange one coloured belt for another every twelve weeks, certainly up to 1st kyu. It is the responsibility of the instructor to prepare the student both physically and psychologically. No student should be put forward to grade if they have **no** chance of passing. A word of advice then to those attempting their first grades: your instructor will have taken you through the physical requirements of basics, kata and kumite. These should be practised at home as well as in the dojō. If uncertainties arise, get him to deal with them early on or "as and when" they occur. It's a good idea to get a book that will compliment his teaching and he will advise you on the most suitable publication. In T.A.S.K. for example, students on a twelve week beginners course go through a process of learning new techniques and recapping on ones learnt in previous lessons. By the eleventh week, they go through a "mock" grading, performing the complete syllabus in class. Any problem areas are attended to and a noticeable air of confidence developed. In the last lesson before the examination, the i's are dotted and the t's crossed and the students know exactly what will be expected of them and perhaps more important – that they can do it.

Mention is made in a light-hearted way, *not* to go to any all-night parties the night before or have a six course lunch thirty minutes prior to the exam. The lesson concludes with some fun things, games or sumo wrestling etc, and they leave the dojō in a conducive frame of mind. In conclusion, the grading examination brings the short-term benefit of a higher degree and an "obi" of a new and different colour. In the long-term, the rewards are less tangible but far more profound. Tests, obstacles, problems, challenges, call them what you will, the fact remains **– life is full of them.**

We all want to be successful and there is nothing wrong with that sentiment but perhaps to fail – just occasionally – is not such a bad thing. Remember, **"he who is always successful is not experienced in knowing how to deal with failure when it comes"**.

THE RELATIONSHIP BETWEEN TEACHER AND STUDENT

In principle, the relationship between teacher and student is the same in the West as it is in the East. The reality differs considerably, and many Japanese students could be forgiven for thinking that Westerners have an attitude problem. Of course they don't, for the Western teacher is viewed by student and layman alike with *different eyes.*

The word for teacher in Japanese is *sensei*, and it's a little difficult to impart the feeling of respect and admiration that Japanese have for one who has been bestowed with this title.
This short story should demonstrate the point.

In the late 'sixties I accompanied Kanazawa sensei to a rendezvous in London with an old Japanese gentleman. I had not seen or heard of this man before, so you can imagine my surprise when, on meeting him, Kanazawa sensei, who was then 6th dan, bowed very low indeed and addressed the man as *"sensei"*. Throughout the long conversation he used the word "sensei" almost constantly and with great reverence. Sitting back in silence, I wondered what grade this master must be, and indeed, what art did he practise? He probably did them all!

On the way home, I just couldn't contain myself any longer. "Sensei," I said, "what grade is that old gentleman?" "No grade," replied Kanazawa sensei. "Then, what martial art does he practise?" "No martial art" came the answer. I paused for a moment. "Then why do you call him 'sensei'?" "Because he is a teacher – **a teacher of life**."

In time, I would come to understand the meaning of that remark – but not then.

Today, the word "sensei" is used for anyone who stands in front of a class. Students grading to black belt, in some cases, almost expect to be called "sensei".

A student of karate should be polite, respectful and courteous towards his sensei. He should have his teacher's welfare at heart and be prepared to protect his honour in both his presence and absence alike.

Most of all – he should be loyal.

THE CASE FOR CHILDREN IN KARATE

Even to the staunch traditionalist, karate training is forever changing and this is perfectly natural as our knowledge of the human body increases.

To the karate teacher, children are not miniature adults. Their physiology differs enormously as too do their levels and types of fitness. Childrens' bones are not fully formed and adult exercises can cause permanent damage. Bearing these points in mind, the case for childrens' involvement in karate cannot be ignored. Twenty years ago, the average karate class consisted of about 2% children and 98% adults. Today, 60% to 70% of students are children under the age of 14. The reason for this massive increase stems largely from, "just how beneficial karate training can be for young people". Most traditional martial arts have the same effect but I speak as a karate teacher only and one who has a very limited knowledge of other disciplines.

Children are taught from the outset that karate is primarily defensive and not offensive. They are taught never to use their fighting skills outside the training hall (dojō), except in cases of extreme provocation and then only to defend. Apart from the physical aspects, everything else practised in the dojō must be practised in the course of their life. For example:

Etiquette: A boy or girl during the first few weeks of their training learns and practises basic etiquette. They learn to be polite and respect their fellow students, instructor and parents. Soon, they become aware that good manners consist of having consideration for other people.

Discipline: Young people react to discipline very well considering how little they seem to get of it on the domestic front. Many parents often absolve themselves of all responsibility in this department, transferring the load to the already overburdened school teacher. Once a child has been disciplined for a short period, he then develops self-discipline and behaves correctly, of his own free will. His concentration is enhanced as he focuses his mind on the job in hand, whether it may be learning a sequence of complicated moves or passing an exam at school. Many parents notice a marked improvement in their childs' powers of concentration once karate training has commenced. Ironically however, very few are prepared to acknowledge publicly that the karate instructor may have been instrumental in achieving this.

In my opinion, children should not be made to think of themselves as failures. These "adults of tomorrow" should be encouraged in everything they do. How many times do you hear a parent shouting at a child, telling him "you're stupid" "you're terrible", "you should be ashamed of yourself". Say them enough and the child will think of himself and grow up, stupid, terrible and ashamed. On the other hand – praise, compliment and encourage him and you will have a child who is confident, well balanced and a pleasure to be with.

Self Confidence: Karate wins hands down on this score every time, but is it any wonder many children lack confidence in themselves? Just look at many parents – they do. From birth, children learn by mimicking the parents' actions. Can you blame a child for being tense and nervous after observing his parents desperate attempts to "make ends meet" and cope with the enormous pressures of 20th century living.

Traditional karate training helps prepare a child for life. I find it enormously encouraging when a mother or father who brings a child to lessons, does not just dump them, and head straight for the nearest pub, but instead, comes in the dojō, sits down and takes an interest in what their child is learning. Children love to perform, especially to the people closest to them and they are far more clever than we give them credit for. How often are "little cries for help" disregarded. Rejection, to a child from questions like "come and play with me", or read, or walk or do anything, can be very hurtful, especially when the child has heard it one hundred times before. Answers like: "I haven't got time", "later", or "I'm busy", do nothing to inspire confidence.

When children come to my karate lessons, I tell them that for the next hour I'm going to treat them like adults. When the lesson is over, they will walk out of the dojō and their parents and the world will treat them again like children. The response I get is nothing short of amazing. Just watching 7-year-olds standing next to grown men and women, learning together is quite something. The children know more is expected from them and with a little encouragement from the teacher, they rise to the occasion.

Fitness: As a method of keeping fit, karate is almost without equal. Many adults find it difficult to stay in good shape, whereas children find it a lot easier, consequently, they enjoy it more. A healthy body promotes a healthy mind.

Self-defence: Growing up in the early 'fifties, apart from scraps that all boys get into, I cannot remember seeing much street violence or hearing of muggings, although I'm sure it must have gone on. Forty years on, things do appear to have changed somewhat. Today, muggings take place in every town in the country. No longer are they the province of the elderly and now young people are considered "fair game". During the last five years we have witnessed the most bloody riots in Toxteth and Brixton with hundreds of innocent people and police officers being assaulted. Add to that "the peaceful protest" against the community charge that left Trafalgar Square looking more like Agincourt, and you have a reasonable case for learning self-defence.

Training for life: The psychological theme running through each lesson epitomises the triumph of good over evil. It encourages a gentlemanly code of conduct and the necessity to maintain standards. Discipline, etiquette and respect for one's elders all have their place in budo, the code of the military man. To relate, communicate and co-exist peaceably with one's fellow man is a worthy ideal worth striving for.

Success at school: Through constant repetition and self-analysis of physical techniques, relative perfection is ultimately acquired. Once this learning technique has become a habit, the principle will automatically be applied to most things by the sub-conscious. Indeed, many parents and school teachers have remarked how their child's powers of concentration have improved since starting karate training. Co-ordination obviously becomes much better as too does the child's awareness factor. The latter without doubt, plays a key role throughout a person's life.

THE MATURE STUDENT

The mature student is a relatively new phenomenon and indeed a welcome one. For this, we have to thank changing attitudes amongst the top teachers of karate-dō during the last thirty years.

Once upon a time, karate, although looking very attractive to most age ranges, succeeded in *keeping* within its ranks only young men between the ages of seventeen and thirty with very few exceptions to the rule.

Karate needed to broaden its parameters to survive and grow. With the massive migration of karate-dō to the west, initiated primarily by the Japan Karate Association (J.K.A.) in the "sixties", the Japanese realised, that in giving westerners a little of what they wanted them to have, they also had to give the west a lot of what westerners wanted. Think about it.

It was all a question of balance and it took some time to get it right. By being too severe, the younger and older members of society were not attracted, or if they were, would quickly fall by the way-side. Apart from that, it was terribly counter productive to their aim, which was to spread the word. Eventually they did it – and most successfully too!

So what appeal does karate-dō have for the older person? Apparently – a great deal.

The mature student is capable of understanding the philosophy behind karate-dō and relating and applying it to his everyday life. His interest in fighting and tournaments is academic at the very best. So he finds the movements and application of kata delightful.

By exercising regularly, he improves his flexibility – already on the decline – becomes fitter and healthier and without doubt, looks and feels much younger.

The threat of arthritis with advancing years has receded, and breathing, the first thing he ever did and the last thing he will ever do, takes on a new significance. Add to that the possibility of research and the study of an art whose origins are lost in antiquity and you have an ideal student, who without doubt, will grace any dojō in the land.

The author expounding the virtues of karate-dō in 1987 to a well-known senior citizen. "I like the idea of a blue belt" she said "but exchanging it in 3 months time for a red one, well – I think I'd have to give that some serious consideration".

309

KARATE vs CANCER 1990

There comes a time in most people's lives when they have a desire to "put something back". "Where" and "how" is often more difficult to answer and the necessary motivation is not always forthcoming. That motivation manifested itself in no uncertain terms in the form of Eddie Whitcher.

Eddie, who had pioneered Shotokan Karate in Great Britain in the early 'sixties was suffering from terminal cancer. Throughout his karate life he had been an inspiration to all. Big in stature and mild in manner he was without doubt an extremely gifted Shotokan Traditionalist. A purist in the true sense of the word seeking neither material gain nor recognition.

Visiting him at the Royal London Hospital with Kanazawa Sensei in November 1989, I was shocked by his frail gaunt appearance. As fellow students in 1967, I had watched him fight the best the J.K.A. had to offer – and beat them. Alas – how could he have known the real enemy would come from within.

Happier times: Eddie Whitcher, the family man. Relaxing at home in early 1988.

KARATE vs CANCER 1990

Professor Williams of the Medical Unit at the Royal London Hospital was in charge of his treatment. He did everything in his power to save Eddie's life – sadly, he failed and I couldn't help but be aware of the frustration being experienced by the medical unit due to lack of finance to fund much needed research into finding a cure for this terrible disease.

It was with much pride that I announced to Professor Williams that the members of T.A.S.K. had unanimously agreed to support his research and a target of £50,000 had been set.

So began the biggest ever fundraising event in martial arts history and "Karate vs Cancer" was born. It would span 9 months and culminate on 30th September 1990 with a massive display of punching at T.A.S.K.'s hombu in Bedford.

Martial artists from up and down the country responded magnificently and special thanks went to S.K.A. and E.S.K.A.

Three proud instructors of the clubs who raised the most money.
1st (centre) Stamford, 2nd (left) Flitwick, 3rd (right) Luton.

KARATE vs CANCER 1990

As the 30th September 1990 drew to a close, it was fitting that Eddie Whitcher's two children, Clinton and Camille, should present Professor Williams with a cheque for £125,000.

In his reply, Professor Norman Williams said: "Eddie Whitcher was a remarkable man. He bore his illness with great courage and fortitude. He brought joy to the people looking after him. His inner strength and his superb family helped him cope."

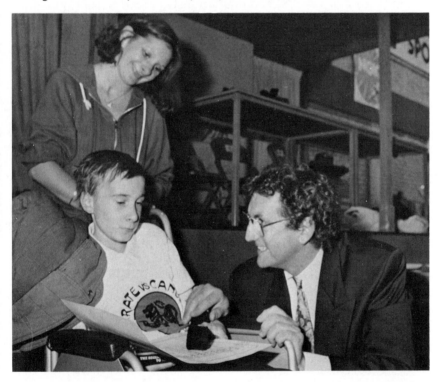

A special guest was 12-year-old James Wightman who's greatest wish was to do karate. James, who had a tumour on the brain, here receives an honorary black belt from Sensei Van Weenen. Two days earlier, James had become blind and Sensei said, "He's the most courageous boy I've ever known". Sadly, a few days later, he died.

KARATE vs CANCER 1990

The final total exceeded the original target 3 times and stands at £158,000.

In the eyes of many of the general public, karate remains just a shade less than respectable, with very little being known of the philosophy concerning "The Way". My sincere hope is that this small effort will have gone some way in redressing the balance and in the process, the image of karate will become a little less tarnished.

Clinton Whitcher (left) and his sister Camille, just prior to presenting the Royal London Hospital with a cheque for £125,000.

Over £4,000 was raised for the widow and children of Eddie Whitcher on a special course put on by seven of his friends.

100 black belts pose for this memorable photograph behind instructors (left to right), Mick Randall, John van Weenen, Mick Nursey, Roger Hall, Harry Jones, Greg Durant and Neville Whitfield.

Taken at Luton in September 1977, H. Kanazawa then 8th Dan, performs his famous butterfly kick after being attacked by E. Whitcher 4th Dan (right) and J. van Weenen 2nd Dan (left).

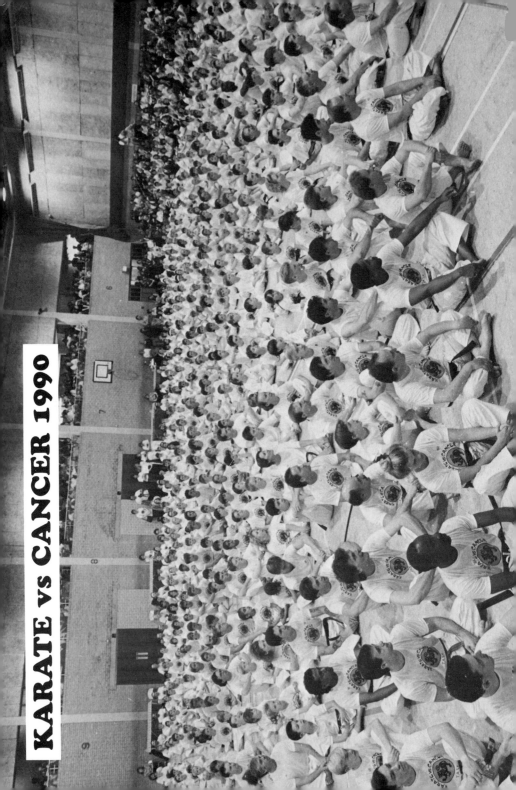

KARATE vs CANCER 1990

A few months before his death Gichin Funakoshi wrote:

"Today, almost everywhere in Japan, I can hear the voices of
karate training.
Now, finally, karate has been introduced to far places abroad. As
I look back over the past forty years to those days in the
beginning when I was first introducing karate with my friends, it
is indeed difficult for me to grasp the present widespread
acceptance of karate. It seems as if it were a different period."

Throughout his life, Funakoshi Sensei preached and taught
traditional values.

I am sure he would take great comfort in knowing they were being
adhered to thirty-three years after his death. What finer tribute to
him could there be, than for 1,000 of his third generation students to
come together, on the other side of the world, motivated, as indeed
he was, by nothing more than a desire to help their fellow man.

Anatomical Charts of Human Musculature
Front

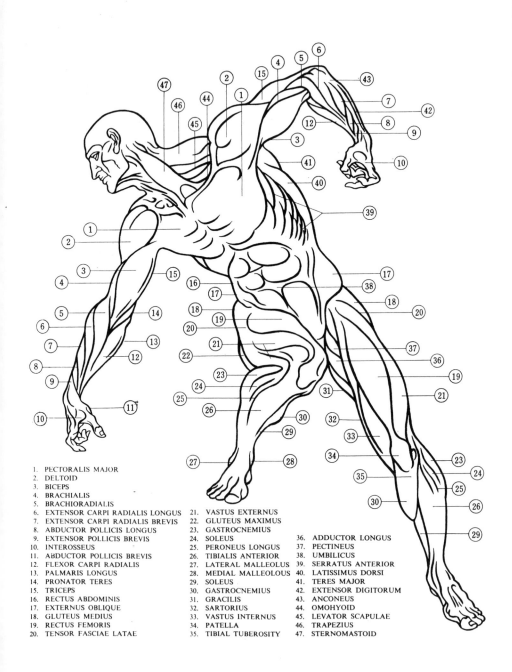

1. PECTORALIS MAJOR
2. DELTOID
3. BICEPS
4. BRACHIALIS
5. BRACHIORADIALIS
6. EXTENSOR CARPI RADIALIS LONGUS
7. EXTENSOR CARPI RADIALIS BREVIS
8. ABDUCTOR POLLICIS LONGUS
9. EXTENSOR POLLICIS BREVIS
10. INTEROSSEUS
11. ABDUCTOR POLLICIS BREVIS
12. FLEXOR CARPI RADIALIS
13. PALMARIS LONGUS
14. PRONATOR TERES
15. TRICEPS
16. RECTUS ABDOMINIS
17. EXTERNUS OBLIQUE
18. GLUTEUS MEDIUS
19. RECTUS FEMORIS
20. TENSOR FASCIAE LATAE

21. VASTUS EXTERNUS
22. GLUTEUS MAXIMUS
23. GASTROCNEMIUS
24. SOLEUS
25. PERONEUS LONGUS
26. TIBIALIS ANTERIOR
27. LATERAL MALLEOLUS
28. MEDIAL MALLEOLOUS
29. SOLEUS
30. GASTROCNEMIUS
31. GRACILIS
32. SARTORIUS
33. VASTUS INTERNUS
34. PATELLA
35. TIBIAL TUBEROSITY

36. ADDUCTOR LONGUS
37. PECTINEUS
38. UMBILICUS
39. SERRATUS ANTERIOR
40. LATISSIMUS DORSI
41. TERES MAJOR
42. EXTENSOR DIGITORUM
43. ANCONEUS
44. OMOHYOID
45. LEVATOR SCAPULAE
46. TRAPEZIUS
47. STERNOMASTOID

318

Back

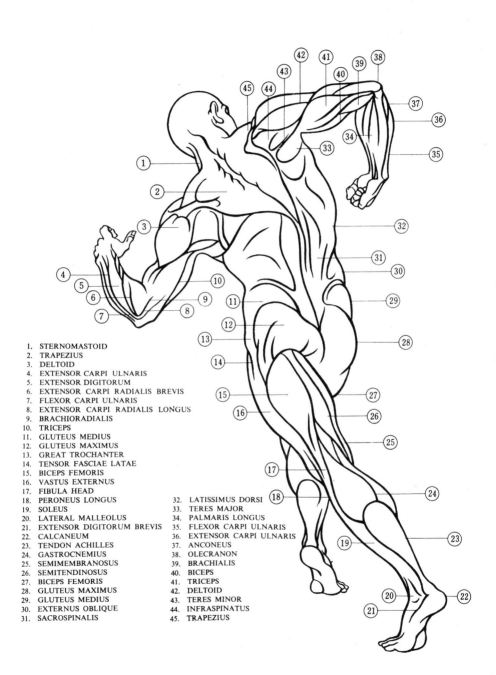

1. STERNOMASTOID
2. TRAPEZIUS
3. DELTOID
4. EXTENSOR CARPI ULNARIS
5. EXTENSOR DIGITORUM
6. EXTENSOR CARPI RADIALIS BREVIS
7. FLEXOR CARPI ULNARIS
8. EXTENSOR CARPI RADIALIS LONGUS
9. BRACHIORADIALIS
10. TRICEPS
11. GLUTEUS MEDIUS
12. GLUTEUS MAXIMUS
13. GREAT TROCHANTER
14. TENSOR FASCIAE LATAE
15. BICEPS FEMORIS
16. VASTUS EXTERNUS
17. FIBULA HEAD
18. PERONEUS LONGUS
19. SOLEUS
20. LATERAL MALLEOLUS
21. EXTENSOR DIGITORUM BREVIS
22. CALCANEUM
23. TENDON ACHILLES
24. GASTROCNEMIUS
25. SEMIMEMBRANOSUS
26. SEMITENDINOSUS
27. BICEPS FEMORIS
28. GLUTEUS MAXIMUS
29. GLUTEUS MEDIUS
30. EXTERNUS OBLIQUE
31. SACROSPINALIS
32. LATISSIMUS DORSI
33. TERES MAJOR
34. PALMARIS LONGUS
35. FLEXOR CARPI ULNARIS
36. EXTENSOR CARPI ULNARIS
37. ANCONEUS
38. OLECRANON
39. BRACHIALIS
40. BICEPS
41. TRICEPS
42. DELTOID
43. TERES MINOR
44. INFRASPINATUS
45. TRAPEZIUS

319

Front

Body structure and vital points

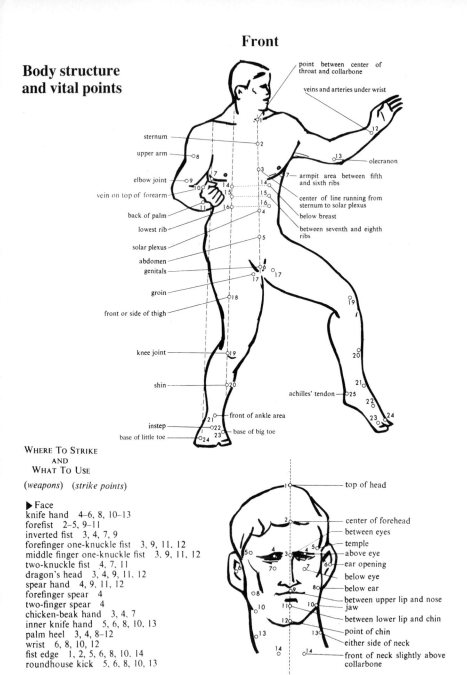

point between center of throat and collarbone

veins and arteries under wrist

sternum
upper arm

olecranon

elbow joint
vein on top of forearm

armpit area between fifth and sixth ribs

center of line running from sternum to solar plexus

back of palm
lowest rib

below breast

between seventh and eighth ribs

solar plexus
abdomen
genitals

groin
front or side of thigh

knee joint

shin

achilles' tendon

front of ankle area
instep
base of little toe

base of big toe

WHERE TO STRIKE
AND
WHAT TO USE

(*weapons*)   (*strike points*)

▶ Face
knife hand   4–6, 8, 10–13
forefist   2–5, 9–11
inverted fist   3, 4, 7, 9
forefinger one-knuckle fist   3, 9, 11, 12
middle finger one-knuckle fist   3, 9, 11, 12
two-knuckle fist   4, 7, 11
dragon's head   3, 4, 9, 11. 12
spear hand   4, 9, 11, 12
forefinger spear   4
two-finger spear   4
chicken-beak hand   3, 4, 7
inner knife hand   5, 6, 8, 10, 13
palm heel   3, 4, 8–12
wrist   6, 8, 10, 12
fist edge   1, 2, 5, 6, 8, 10. 14
roundhouse kick   5, 6, 8, 10, 13

top of head

center of forehead
between eyes
temple
above eye
ear opening
below eye
below ear
between upper lip and nose
jaw
between lower lip and chin
point of chin
either side of neck
front of neck slightly above collarbone

The primary vital spots fall on a straight line midway in the human body and include the forehead, the upper lip, the solar plexus, and the genitals. The secondary vital points fall on straight lines centering on the temples and include the spots below the ears and the spots below the armpits. The tertiary vital spots fall on two lines midway between the primary line and the two secondary lines and include the ribs, spleen, and abdomen.

Back

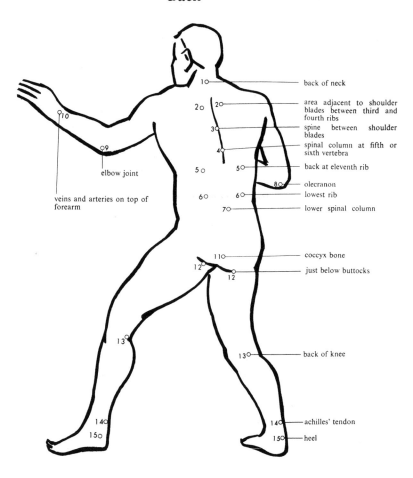

1	back of neck
2	area adjacent to shoulder blades between third and fourth ribs
3	spine between shoulder blades
4	spinal column at fifth or sixth vertebra
5	back at eleventh rib
8	olecranon
6	lowest rib
7	lower spinal column
11	coccyx bone
12	just below buttocks
13	back of knee
14	achilles' tendon
15	heel

10 — veins and arteries on top of forearm

9 — elbow joint

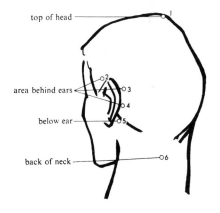

top of head — 1

area behind ears — 2, 3

below ear — 5

back of neck — 6

WHERE TO STRIKE
AND
WHAT TO USE

(*weapons*) (*strike points*)

▶ Front view
knife hand   7, 14–16
forefist   2–7
inverted fist   3, 4, 7, 14–16
forefinger one-knuckle fist   1, 4
middle finger one-knuckle fist   1, 4
dragon's head   1
spear hand   1, 3, 4
forefinger spear   1, 3, 4
two-finger spear   1, 3, 4
inner knife hand   1, 7
palm heel   3–7
wrist   7, 14–16
fist edge   7, 14–16
roundhouse kick   1, 7, 14–16

knee kick   1, 6, 8, 17
front kick   3–6, 14–16
ankle kick   19, 21
heel   21–24
knife foot   4, 5, 6, 14–16

▶ Back view
knife hand   1
forefist   1, 5, 6
elbow   1–6
wrist   1–7
roundhouse kick,   5–7
front kick   11, 12

▶ Back of head
forefist   2–6
inverted fist   2–6
wrist   2–5
fist edge   1–6

321

1-100 ENGLISH – JAPANESE

1 – ICHI	35 – SANJYU GO	69 – ROKUJYU KU
2 – NI	36 – SANJYU ROKU	70 – SHICHIJYU
3 – SAN	37 – SANJYU SHICHI	71 – SHICHIJYU ICHI
4 – SHI	38 – SANJYU HACHI	72 – SHICHIJYU NI
5 – GO	39 – SANJYU KU	73 – SHICHIJYU SAN
6 – ROKU	40 – YONJYU	74 – SHICHIJYU SHI
7 – SHICHI	41 – YONJYU ICHI	75 – SHICHIJYU GO
8 – HACHI	42 – YONJYU NI	76 – SHICHIJYU ROKU
9 – KU	43 – YONJYU SAN	77 – SHICHIJYU SHICHI
10 – JYU	44 – YONJYU SHI	78 – SHICHIJYU HACHI
11 – JYU ICHI	45 – YONJYU GO	79 – SHICHIJYU KU
12 – JYU NI	46 – YONJYU ROKU	80 – HACHIJYU
13 – JYU SAN	47 – YONJYU SHICHI	81 – HACHIJYU ICHI
14 – JYU SHI	48 – YONJYU HACHI	82 – HACHIJYU NI
15 – JYU GO	49 – YONJYU KU	83 – HACHIJYU SAN
16 – JYU ROKU	50 – GOJYU	84 – HACHIJYU SHI
17 – JYU SHICHI	51 – GOJYU ICHI	85 – HACHIJYU GO
18 – JYU HACHI	52 – GOJYU NI	86 – HACHIJYU ROKU
19 – JYU KU	53 – GOJYU SAN	87 – HACHIJYU SHICHI
20 – NIJYU	54 – GOJYU SHI	88 – HACHIJYU HACHI
21 – NIJYU ICHI	55 – GOJYU GO	89 – HACHIJYU KU
22 – NIJYU NI	56 – GOJYU ROKU	90 – KYUJYU
23 – NIJYU SAN	57 – GOJYU SHICHI	91 – KYUJYU ICHI
24 – NIJYU SHI	58 – GOJYU HACHI	92 – KYUJYU NI
25 – NIJYU GO	59 – GOJYU KU	93 – KYUJYU SAN
26 – NIJYU ROKU	60 – ROKUJYU	94 – KYUJYU SHI
27 – NIJYU SHICHI	61 – ROKUJYU ICHI	95 – KYUJYU GO
28 – NIJYU HACHI	62 – ROKUJYU NI	96 – KYUJYU ROKU
29 – NIJYU KU	63 – ROKUJYU SAN	97 – KYUJYU SHICHI
30 – SANJYU	64 – ROKUJYU SHI	98 – KYUJYU HACHI
31 – SANJYU ICHI	65 – ROKUJYU GO	99 – KYUJYU KU
32 – SANJYU NI	66 – ROKUJYU ROKU	100 – HYAKU
33 – SANJYU SAN	67 – ROKUJYU SHICHI	
34 – SANJYU SHI	68 – ROKUJYU HACHI	

RECOMMENDED READING

Title: Karate-Dō Nyūmon
Author: Gichin Funakoshi
Publisher: Kodansha International

*Title: Karate-Dō Kyohan
Author: Gichin Funakoshi
Publisher: Kodansha – UK Ward Lock Publications Ltd

*Title: Karate-Dō: My Way of Life
Author: Gichin Funakoshi
Publisher: Kodansha International

Title: Dynamic Karate
Author: Masatoshi Nakayama
Publisher: Ward Lock Publications Ltd

Title: The Heart of Karate-Dō
Author: Shigeru Egami
Publisher: Kodansha International

*Title: Karate's History and Traditions
Author: Bruce A. Haines
Publisher: Charles E. Tuttle & Co

Title: Diary of the Way
Author: Ira Lerner
Publisher: The Ridge Press

Title: Dynamic Powers of Karate
Author: Hirokazu Kanazawa
Publisher: Dragon Books

Title: Karate – The Art of Empty Hand Fighting
Author: Hidetaka Nishiyama & Richard C. Brown
Publisher: Charles E. Tuttle & Co

Title: Moving Zen
Author: C. W. Nicol
Publisher: Willian Morrow & Co. Inc, New York

* Compulsory reading within T.A.S.K. for all attempting black belt rank.

USEFUL NAMES AND ADDRESSES

Martial Arts Commission, 1st Floor, Broadway House, 15-16 Deptford Broadway, London SE8 4PE. Tel: 081-691 3433.
Traditional Association of Shotokan Karate (T.A.S.K.), c/o The Bunyan Centre, Mile Road, Bedford. Tel: (0234) 364481.
All enquiries for membership to T.A.S.K. from individuals or associations should be addressed to: Mr E. McClagish, T.A.S.K. General Secretary at the above address.

IN CONCLUSION

After reading this book, for whatever it is worth, my sincere wish is that it will have contributed in some measure to your knowledge of Shotokan Karate and encouraged you to continue with the study of Karate-Dō.

As a teacher of the art for many years now, I have seen a great number of people come, but alas – a great number of people go. Losing students is terribly disappointing, especially when considering the tremendous potential many of them appear to have.

First to go is the "undesirable", thankfully eliminating himself, closely followed by many of the "Instant Kickers". Those who have a natural aptitude for the physical accomplishments of Karate but quite early on, find it "All too easy" – and give up, without really having ever TRIED. Ultimately, that Western adage would seem to apply – "You can lead a horse to water . . ."

So who are the people who remain to become the teachers and masters of tomorrow? The answer to that question is, apart from a handful of naturally talented people – ordinary folk!

The art of Karate holds a mystical appeal for many. Initially perhaps, the ability of a man to put his hand through a brick and later the thought of becoming invincible, repelling any attack by any number of assailants. For the average man to acquire this knowledge and become "extraordinary", is perhaps, in the first instance an enthralling notion and an opportunity too good to miss. Of course, after several months of serious training the student realises he may never become a "Superman" and quite probably doesn't want to either. For the idea will be dawning, that the continued practise of basic fundamentals is having an effect on the way he sees, feels and behaves towards other people and at this point, he has begun his journey, along "The Way".

The physical movements of punching, kicking, striking and blocking performed repeatedly, are but a vehicle needed to transport the traveller along "The Way" to his appointed destination. The journey is a gradual one and cannot be undergone in a few months. There is no substitute for time – and that is what it takes.

Karate has been described as a "Moving Zen" and I personally believe it is akin to religion. It is about helping people, doing someone a good turn – not a bad one and above all humility. How clear are the words of "The Dōjō Kun", if we can only live up to them.

Unfortunately, we are human, therefore imperfect, but the fact remains – it's not THE STYLE that is important but the way in which THE MAN conducts himself and sets an example for others to follow.

Karate-Dō, practised sincerely, will build confidence, promote fitness, improve fighting ability and enhance longevity of life but these are small measure compared to the "Real" benefits awaiting you.

GLOSSARY

JAPANESE	PRONUNCIATION	ENGLISH	PAGES
Kumite	(koo-me-teh)	Sparring	-
Jiyū Kumite	(gee-you koo-me-teh)	Free sparring	-
Jōdan	(joe-dahn)	Upper level	-
Jūji Uke	(jew-gee oo-kay)	'X' block	70
Ka	(kah)	Person or practitioner	-
Kage Uke	(kah-gay oo-kay)	Hooking block	-
Kage Zuki	(kah-gay zoo-key)	Hooking punch	32
Kakato	(kah-kah-toe)	Heel	-
Kakiwake Uke	(kah-key-wah-kay oo-kay)	Wedge block	76
Kamikaze	(kah-me-kah-zay)	Literally: Divine wind. World War II suicide pilots	-
Kankū	(kahn-koo)	To look at the sky	-
Kara	(kah-rah)	Empty – Chinese	-
Kata	(kah-tah)	Formal exercise	99–201
Keage	(kay-ah-geh)	Snap	82
Keitō Uke	(kay-toe oo-kay)	Chicken-head wrist block	98
Kekomi	(kay-koh-me)	Thrust	84
Keri	(kay-rhee)	(geri) Kick	78
Ki	(key)	Inner power – Spirit	-
Kiai	(key-i)	Shout used to unite Ki and Physical	-
Kiba Dachi	(kay-bah dah-chee)	Straddle or horse-riding stance	158–159
Kihon Ippon Kumite	(key-hone eepone koo-me-teh)	Basic one-step sparring	225
Kime	(key-may)	Focus	-
Kizami Zuki	(key-zah-me zoo-key)	Front snap punch	-
Kin Geri	(as kith and kin geh-rhee)	Groin kick	-
Kokutsu Dachi	(koh-koo-tsue dah-chee)	Back stance	186
Koshi	(ko-shi)	Ball of foot	92
Kumade	(koo-mah-deh)	Bear hand	-
Kumite	(koo-meh-teh)	Sparring	202–257
Kun	(kun. 'u' as 'ou' in 'could')	Oath	258
Kyu	(quew)	Rank below black belt	-
Ma-ai	(mah-aye)	Distancing	225
Mae	(mah-eh)	Front	-
Mae Geri	(mah-eh geh-rhee)	Front kick	80
Makiwara	(mah-key-wha-rha)	Striking post	-
Mawashi Geri	(mah-wha-she geh-rhee)	Roundhouse kick	86
Mawashi Zuki	(mah-wha-she zoo-key)	Roundhouse punch	24
Mawate	(mah-wha-teh)	Turn	-
Migi	(me-ghee)	Right side	-
Mika Zuki Geri	(me-kah zoo-key geh-rhee)	Crescent kick	90–92
Mizu No Kokoro	(me-zoo-no ko-ko-ro)	Mind like water	185
Mokuso	(mo ['orange'] koo-so ['orange'])	Meditation	258
Morote Uke	(moe-row-teh oo-kay)	Augmented block	64
Morote Zuki	(moe-row-teh zoo-key)	Augmented punch	20
Nagashi Uke	(nah-gah-she oo-kay)	Stepping block	-
Naha-te	(nah-hah-tay)	Okinawan school of karate	-
Nakadaka-Ippon-Ken	(nar-kah-dah-kar eepone-ken)	Middle-finger one-knuckle fist	-
Nami-Ashi	(nah-mee ah-she)	Inside leg block	-
Neko Ashi Dachi	(neh-koh ah-she dah-she)	Cat stance	248
Nidan Geri	(nee-dahn geh-rhee)	Double kick	-
Nihon Nukite	(nee-hone noo-key-teh)	Two-finger spear hand	-
Nukite	(noo-key-teh)	Spear hand straight thrust	137
Obi	(o ['orange']-bee)	Belt-sash	-
Oi Zuki	(oh-ee zoo-key)	Stepping punch	16
Okinawa-te	(o-kin-ar-wah-teh)	Okinawan school of karate	-
Rei	(ray)	Bow	-
Ren Zuki	(wren zoo-key)	Alternate punching	174
Ryu	(ree-you)	School (of karate)	275
Sambon Kumite	(sam-bon ['orange'] koo-me-tey)	3-step sparring	219
Seiken	(say-ken)	Forefist	12
Seiza	(say-zar)	Kneeling position (meditation posture)	258
Sempai	(sem-pie)	Senior	-
Sensei	(sen-say)	Teacher	-

JAPANESE	PRONUNCIATION	ENGLISH	PAGES
Seppuku	(sep-poo-koo)	Ritual suicide	-
Shihan	(she-hahn)	Master (6th dan and above)	-
Shiro	(she-roe)	White	-
Shizentai	(she-zen-tah-ee)	Natural stance	-
Shutō	(shoe-toe)	Knife hand	36
Shutō Uchi	(shoe-toe oo-chee)	Knife-hand strike	36–37
Shutō Uke	(shoe-toe oo-kay)	Knife-hand block	66
Sochin	(saw-chin)	Takes name from Immovable stance (formal exercise)	-
Sokutō	(sow-koo-toe)	Foot edge	82–84
Soto Ude Uke	(so-toh oo-day oo-kay)	Outside forearm block	60
Taikyoku	(tar-eek-yo-koo)	First cause	-
Taikyoku Shodan	(tar-eek-yo-koo sho-dahn)	First cause (formal exercise)	101
Tai Sabaki	(tar-ee sah-bah-kee)	Body shifting	-
T.A.S.K.		Traditional Association of Shotokan Karate	261
Tate Shutō Uke	(tah-teh shoe-toe oo-kay)	Vertical knife-hand block	68
Te	(teh)	Hand	-
Teishō	(tay-sho)	Palm heel	-
Teishō Uchi	(tay-sho oo-chee)	Palm-heel strike	-
Teishō Uke	(tay-sho oo-kay)	Palm-heel block	172
Tekki Nidan*	(teh-key knee-dahn)	2nd level	-
Tekki Sandan*	(teh-key sahn-dahn)	3rd level	-
Tekki Shodan*	(teh-key sho-dahn)	1st level	-
Tettsui	(tett-sooie)	Bottom fist	-
Tettsui Uchi	(tett-sooie oo-chee)	Bottom-fist strike	40
Tobi	(tow-be)	Jumping	-
Tsuki	(tsue-key)	Punching	12
Uchi	(oo-chee)	Strike	34
Uchi Ude Uke	(oo-chee oo-day oo-kay)	Inside block (forearm)	62
Ude	(oo-day)	Forearm	-
Uke	(oo-kay)	Block	56
Unsu	(oon-soo)	Hands of the cloud (formal exercise)	-
Ura Zuki	(oo-rah zoo-key)	Close punch	26
Uraken	(oo-rah ken)	Back fist	42
Ushiro Empi	(oo-she-row en-pee)	Reverse elbow	-
Ushiro Geri	(oo-she-row geh-rhee)	Back kick	88
Ushiro Mawashi Geri	(oo-she-row mah-wha-she geh-rhee)	Back roundhouse kick	94
Washide	(wah-she-deh)	Eagle hand (beak)	-
Wankan	(wahn-kahn)	Shortest shotokan formal exercise	-
Yama Zuki	(yah-mah zoo-key)	'U' punch	30
Yame	(yah-may)	Stop – finish	-
Yoi	(as in 'boy')	Ready	-
Yoko	(yoh-koh)	Side	-
Yoko Empi Uchi	(yoh-koh en-pee oo-chee)	Side elbow strike	52
Yoko Geri	(yoh-koh geh-rhee)	Side kick	82–84
Zazen	(zar-zen)	Seated meditation	-
Zen	(zen)	Form of Buddhism based on meditation	-
Zenkutsu Dachi	(zen-koo-tsue dah-chee)	Front stance	242
Zuki	(zoo-key)	Punch	12

*Tekki means horse riding. These 3 formal exercises take their name from the Straddle stance (Kiba Dachi)

TASK FORCE
ALBANIA

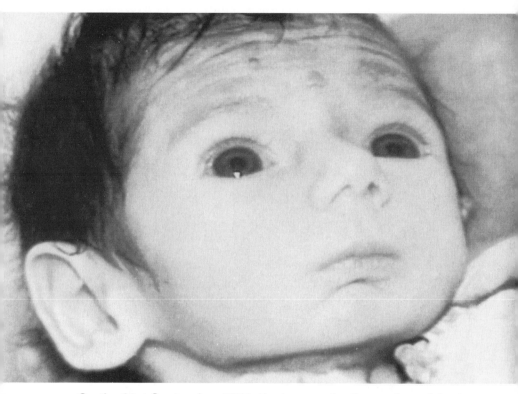

On the 21st September 1991, the image of a tiny malnourished Albanian girl was shown on British television for the first time. The picture, taken by Bhasker Solanki and Bill Hamilton of the BBC, had quite an incredible effect on the British people and in particular, the author of this book. By the time **Jessica's** story had reached our television screens, she was already **dead**, weighing at five months one pound less than her birth weight.

Two weeks later, I was leaving Heathrow bound for Tirana, the capital of Albania and it would be the Albanian Democratic Party Leader, Dr. Sali Berisha, who would meet me at Rhinas Airport. During the next seven days, he showed me his country and his people, still dominated as they had been for fifty years by Communism, most of it under the tyrannical dictatorship of Enver Hoxha.

Returning to England, determined to do something, I enlisted the help of T.A.S.K. The members responded immediately and within days, the new charity **"Task Force Albania"** was formed and a campaign to transport aid to Albania quickly gathered momentum.

Three months later, after having set up collection points in over **100 towns and cities** in the U.K., the largest single convoy ever assembled in peace time, departed on 26th January 1992 from Bedford.

The President of Albania, Dr. Sali Berisha with the author.

It comprised of twenty thirty-eight tonne juggernauts, carrying over **seven hundred tonnes** of food, clothing and medical supplies to Europe's poorest country.

The trip, although extremely hazardous, was tremendously successful with **95%** of all the aid reaching the Albanian people. The support team of thirty T.A.S.K. students and instructors were superb and played a major role in achieving our objectives.

In March 1992, the Democratic Party won a landslide victory over the Communists and their leader, **Dr. Sali Berisha**, became the President of Albania.
Now the real work could begin and I felt an irresistible compulsion to play a very small part in bringing Albania into the 20th century.

330

Hospital conditions were appalling and the health service under the Communists had been decimated. Doctors and surgeons like all other Albanian nationals were forbidden to travel abroad, resulting in a tremendous thirst for western knowledge. The course of action was obvious.

Suppose I could bring some of the best English doctors to Albania and vice versa. At that time, it all seemed somewhat ambitious with the problems of language, communication, visas, passports and finance to be overcome. Charles Hutton, director of the New Victoria hospital in Kingston-Upon-Thames, London, responded magnificently, as did surgeon Nick Jacobs, anaesthetist John Maynard and O.D.A. John Gurrin.

The "New Victoria" team flew to Tirana in May 1992 at their own expense and successfully performed complicated eye surgery on **twenty orphaned children**, many of whom were blind or suffering from severe squints, cataracts and glaucoma.

Correspondingly, four months later, **"Task Force Albania"** brought three eminent doctors specialising in Pediatrics, Ophthalmology and Anaesthesia to London to study western technology at the top London teaching hospitals. So successful was it, that all three, on their return to Tirana, conducted seminars in their own field, attracting doctors from the length and breadth of Albania.

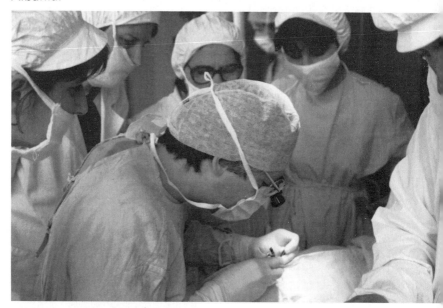

Dr. Nick Jacobs performing eye surgery in Tirana on Anila, a blind orphan girl.

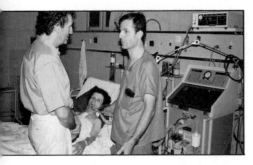

Dr. Roland Xhaxho on 18 June 1992 receiving Albania's first jet ventilator from John van Weenen. It arrived just in time to save Fatime Hasani's life, suffering from a collapsed lung condition.

Children from Shkodra's "Teufik G'yli" orphanage in their new clothes from England, are given "sweets" for the first time.

Huddled together on cold stone floors in their own excreta, were the children of Shkodra's mentally handicapped institute comforted to the best of her ability by Anila, aged 14, lice ridden and blind from birth.

A jubilant Prof. Sulejman Zhugli head of Tirana's ophthamological department, receiving Albania's first "Perimeter" brought from England by T.F.A.

As she is today, pictured visiting England, thanks to a good samaritan, Mrs Barbara Locke.

"Task Force Albania" received official charity status in November 1992 and Esther Rantzen very kindly saw fit to include us in her BBC December **"Hearts of Gold"** television programme.

With Albania celebrating **"Christmas"** for the first time in fifty years, christians were jubilant to say the least and although in his infinite wisdom, Enver Hoxha had **"abolished God and Christianity"**, he failed to remove it from the hearts and minds of a vast number of people.

Fortunately, like **Edith Durham** the English anthropologist before me, I had developed a "fatal attraction" for "Malesia E Madhe". No aid whatsoever had gone to this part of northern Albania and its tribal people were desperate. Every truck we could muster, took much needed food, clothing and medical supplies to Bajze, Koplik, Tamara, Shkodra and Vermosh and every item was donated free of charge by the people of England.

The children of Kingsbrook Middle School in Bedford "loading up" their aid.

T.F.A. trucks arriving on Albanian soil at Durres after a long trip from Trieste by ferry.

Finally, the "well guarded" warehouse in Bajze.

In March 1993, Bedfordshire schoolchildren's campaign to clothe their Albanian counterparts received official backing from the Minister of Education **Baroness Blatch**. The children's generosity had to be seen to be believed, all started by pupils of Kingsbrook Middle School in Bedford.

Just prior to this, I had the wonderful opportunity to visit Calcutta to meet Albania's most famous citizen - **Mother Teresa**. No words can adequately express my admiration and respect for this tiny, frail 83 year old lady who arrived in 1937 in Entally, a suburb of Calcutta, with just **a five rupee note - and a lot of faith!** Never once asking for government backing or church funding, she has managed to build a vast network of missionaries of charity, over 600 in 108 countries worldwide. To the world's destitute, she gives **hope**. To the poor, afflicted and diseased she shows **love**. In these troubled times in which we live, she restores faith in human nature, without doubt - **a living saint**.

Talking to her in April 93, having just returned from the Great Highlands after delivering medical aid with the invaluable help of TASK members Alan Bristow, Azad Kumar and Alan Blake, I noticed she was troubled.

In June 1992, President Berisha bestowed upon John the nation's highest civilian honour, "The Order of Mother Teresa". He very proudly accepted it on behalf of all Karate-Ka from Albania's most famous citizen herself.

A major problem for her now that her organisation has grown so large, is getting from country to country. She has to rely totally on charity and as she never asks for it - it isn't **ALWAYS** forthcoming.

Perhaps I should have a word with British Airways on my return to London. "Would you really?" she replied. "That would be wonderful". I have to say, not knowing anyone at B.A. and starting from scratch, was a shade daunting but I was determined not to be fobbed off by an army of secretaries.

A week later, from executive level came the answer I had been hoping for. British Airways would provide Mother Teresa and her travelling companion with **FREE** 1st class tickets, to travel at will on any British Airways route, anywhere in the world, for the rest of her life. I thought to myself, "Mother will be pleased".

Gichin Funakoshi

Mother Teresa

The other day, whilst reading Funakoshi Sensei's **"Karate Dō Kyōhan"**, I came to the chapter entitled **"Maxims for the Trainee"**. Although I had read this piece many times before, a couple of lines seemed to take on a whole new meaning.

"Make benevolence your lifelong duty. This surely is an important mission. It is a lifelong effort, truly a long journey".

How strange I thought. In one sentence he had captured the whole meaning of **Karate Dō**, whilst epitomising the long struggle and unselfish dedication of a certain, **rather special, Loreto Nun.**

Bedfordshire Times Series, D

(0234) 363101. Fax: (0234) 325721

Prime Minister backs appeal for Albania

PRIME Minister John Major has given his backing to the TASK Force Albania mercy mission from Bedford following an appeal by co-ordinator John Van Weenen.